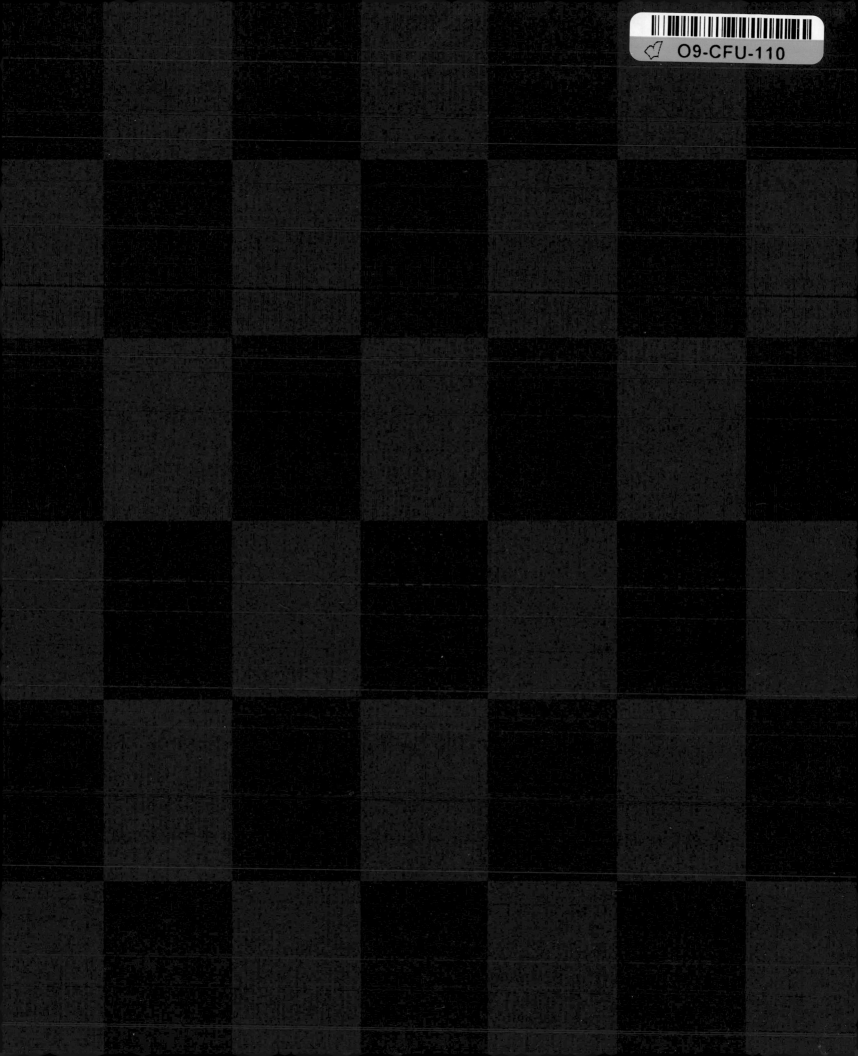

foreword

Jean-Christophe and I go back a long way. We have been like brothers since we were both starting out in the cooking world, and there's a lot of mutual respect. When I first met him, he seemed like a man obsessed, with his food and where he was going... and he's still like that.

Since he first hit the London stage he has really played to his own audience and now, with his own group of restaurants and no one to clip his wings, he is free to be himself and explore his exceptional talent.

He's a very honest person — what you see with Jean is what you get — but he is also very complex, and his honesty and complexity are reflected in his food.

Sometimes I worry that he has bitten off more than he can chew, but then he's still chewing...

Marco Pierre White

novel

your place or

Clarkson Potter/Publishers
New York

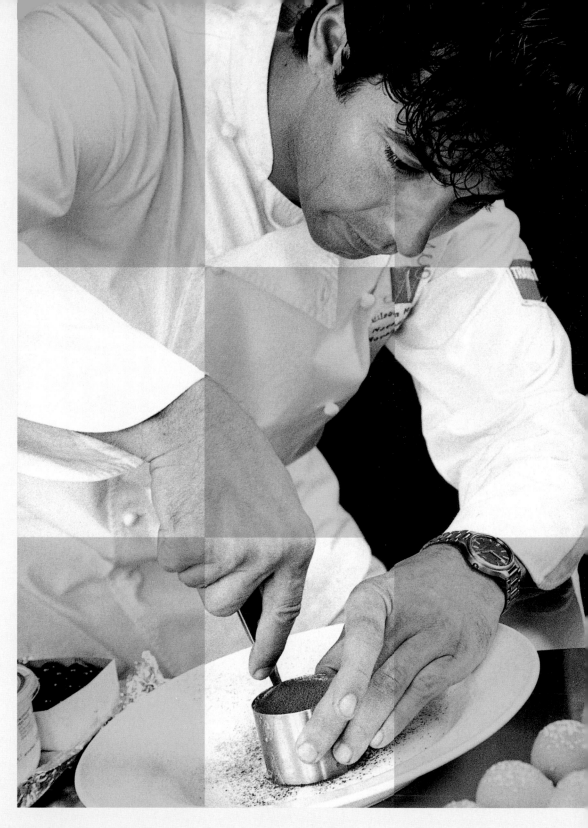

cooking at home with restaurant style

Jean-Christophe Novelli with Sheila Keating
Photography by Jean Cazals

For the three women I love: my mum,
who is a better cook than me, my daughter
Christina, and Anzelle. JCN

Art Director: Mary Evans
Editorial Director: Anne Furniss
Editor & Project Manager: Lewis Esson
Design: Paul Welti
Photography: Jean Cazals
Production: Candida Jackson

Published by Clarkson N. Potter/Publishers, 201 East
50th Street, New York, New York 10022. Member of
the Crown Publishing Group.

Originally published in Great Britain by
Quadrille Publishing Ltd in 1998.

Random House, Inc.
New York, Toronto, London, Sydney, Auckland

www.randomhouse.com

CLARKSON N. POTTER, POTTER, and colophon are trademarks
of Clarkson N. Potter, Inc.

Printed in Germany

Library of Congress Cataloging-in-Publication Data is
available upon request.

ISBN 0-609-60436-8

10 9 8 7 6 5 4 3 2 1

First American Edition

Note: Nature is unpredictable, as are
ovens, so it is impossible to be unequivocal
about cooking times. Your fish might be a
little thicker than mine, your quail eggs a
little larger; I use gas, you might use
electricity...

Remember, too, that no one ever became a
chef in a day, or stopped learning. The fun
of cooking is adapting, developing,
experimenting.

contents

author's
preface

Suivant mon humeur — according to my mood, my passion — is the description that accompanies the dish of pig's feet on all my menus, a dish that is prepared in a different way each day. When critics write about my restaurants it is the thing they always pick up on, perhaps because it sums up my whole attitude to cooking, in fact my whole attitude to life.

For me nothing ever stays still. I am always searching for the next idea, the next adventure...to stand still is to stagnate. Even while I am perfecting one dish I am already thinking of how I can take it a stage further, or take apart its elements and reassemble them in another dish. Even before I opened my first restaurant, in my mind I was already planning the next three.

People say to me, "Slow down, you can't do all these things, take your time," but I say, "You don't know me." I live my life through instinct, by trusting what my heart tells me to do, then throwing myself into a project, without sleep, without thinking about anything else, until it is perfect.

I am not completely crazy, however. I know that to have success you must have a foundation that is solid and sure. In my restaurants I need the people who have cooked with me and shared experiences over the years — people I can trust. The same principle holds with my cooking. I may have a reputation for taking risks with daring

combinations of flavors, but at the heart of my dishes are sure and tested recipes, built on the principles of flavor and texture and the true marriage of ingredients. Once I have these recipes, then I can take chances, play with new flavors, be extravagant.

To simple recipes that you could cook at home every day for the family, I add new sauces and garnishes to build up more elaborate dishes, refined and presented in restaurant style, that you can try for special occasions. When you have the confidence to experiment and improvise for yourself, that is when cooking becomes a real joy. I hope that this book will help you to begin simply, then let your imagination soar. That is what I do at my place; why not try it at yours...*suivant votre humeur.*

box of tricks

From a simple dish, many more can grow — variations, elaborations, whole families of dishes that can be served as first or main courses. I think I am quite unusual in that when I first begin to think about a dish, I start with the shape, not the flavor. I sketch a design, and when I am happy with that, then I start to fill in the tastes and colors, building up the ideas until I have something that satisfies all the senses.

Often I will start with one of my trusted recipes, then I open up my box of tricks and add sauces, oils, powders, and garnishes, as a child might experiment with building blocks. I love to watch people's faces when they see a dish, particularly a dessert, presented in a dramatic and unusual way, with springs made from caramel or a cigar-shaped *tuile*. Of course, the way a dish looks is only one element of its success. If something looks pretty, but tastes of nothing, what is the point? What we look for in most of our garnishes and decorative touches is that intensity of flavor that can be built up to give a dish three or four dimensions in terms of taste. Often the simplest techniques can do just that.

Imagine, you take two ingredients, basil leaves and some good olive oil, and you blitz them together. It takes — what? — two minutes, but the result is something so intensely flavorsome you wonder why you never used it before. We make many of our favorite oils and garnishes from things that other kitchens might discard: for example, instead of throwing away orange peel after you have taken the juice from the fruit, we make a powder with it for sprinkling on pan-fried scallops or plainly cooked fish. What does it cost? Nothing. From that humble ingredient you can create a little bit of magic. You might think it is a lot of work to turn orange peel into a concentrated powder, but what do you really have to do? You just blanch and dry the peel, dust it with a little salt and confectioners' sugar, and leave it in the oven on as low a setting as possible for a few hours until the moisture has all evaporated. Then you grind it in a food processor. To make dried fruit or tomato or eggplant slices for eye-catching decoration you follow a similar process.

I think what sometimes makes the difference between the professional kitchen and the home kitchen is this emphasis on concentrated flavors. As a chef you season constantly, by instinct, but you also spend time reducing sauces again and again until you are left with pure intensity of flavor. The sauces don't have to be complicated: just to reduce some fresh orange juice to a syrup gives an extraordinarily powerful flavor.

For me, oils, juices, reductions, and powders are extra condiments, that can heighten the taste sensation of a dish instantly, and you will find them cropping up again and again in the recipes that follow. The beauty of them is that they can mostly be put together in advance and kept in the refrigerator or the pantry. They then form the basis of a valuable box of tricks that you can open at any time. Perhaps you are broiling a piece of fish; then why not dribble around some concentrated sun-dried tomato juice and finish with a garnish of dried tomato? Instantly you have something that will taste and look a little different, just that bit more impressive.

Finally, I should mention stocks and demi-glace, which chefs make every day and take for granted. We prepare meat stock in the classic way by simmering roasted bones over a long time with aromatic vegetables. Fish stock is made by simmering bones, trimmings, and herbs for only about 20 minutes, otherwise it becomes bitter. I recommend you make your own stock — partly because it is a very satisfying thing to do (I haven't given recipes as I am sure you can readily find them elsewhere.) If you don't have time, look for a good-quality ready-made stock. Where demi-glace is mentioned, this is stock reduced down to the consistency of a sauce, which can be combined with other ingredients or dribbled over a dish to add an extra dimension of intense flavor. It is available from gourmet specialty shops.

oils & reductions

Orange and Cardamom Reduction

It is amazing what depth and intensity of flavor you can get from simply reducing fresh orange juice in a pan with some cardamom pods very, very slowly until it becomes thick and syrupy. This reduction adds a vibrant flavor to simple broiled fish, but I have also used it in all sorts of other ways: I have poured it over a dish of puréed carrots, then glazed this under the broiler, or I have used it (without the garlic) as a syrup for poaching fruit like apples to serve with Pain Perdu (see page 156).

You could even push vanilla beans through the center of some bananas, dip them in the orange reduction (again without the garlic), then roast them briefly in the oven and serve them with some crème pâtissière, between two layers of puff pastry.

makes about ¼ cup

1¼ cups freshly squeezed orange juice
4 cardamom pods
1 garlic clove, split

1 Pass the orange juice through a fine sieve into a pan and add the cardamom pods and garlic.
2 Reduce very slowly until thick and syrupy. Leave to cool and store in the refrigerator.
3 Bring to room temperature before serving.

Orange, Vanilla, and Cardamom Infused Oil

makes about 1¼ cups

1¼ cups freshly squeezed orange juice
4 cardamom pods
1 garlic clove, split
½ vanilla bean
1 cup extra-virgin olive oil

1 Make the orange and cardamom reduction as left.
2 While the reduction is still warm, mix in the seeds from the vanilla bean and the olive oil.
3 Leave for 24 hours to infuse.

Herb Oil

I often add this to mashed potatoes with a little cream and butter.

makes about 1 cup

1 bunch of basil, cilantro, or chives
1 cup extra-virgin olive oil

1 Dip the herbs in boiling water for 1 second, refresh in ice water, and drain.
2 Purée in a blender, then dribble in the olive oil at little at a time until well blended.
3 Strain through cheesecloth.

Chorizo Oil

makes about 5 cups

1 Spanish chorizo sausage, thinly sliced
4 garlic cloves, minced
4½ cups extra-virgin olive oil
4 bay leaves
2 sprigs of rosemary
2 sprigs of thyme
freshly ground salt and black pepper

1 Fry the chorizo and garlic gently in a little oil.
2 Stir in the herbs and season.
3 Transfer to a sterilized jar and cover with the rest of the oil. Cover tightly. Keep for at least 24 hours before use, and then up to 1 week in the refrigerator.

Sherry Dressing

makes about 1½ cups

1 cup olive oil
3 tablespoons sherry vinegar
1 tablespoon clear honey
1 teaspoon grain mustard
1 garlic clove, minced
freshly ground salt and pepper

Combine all the ingredients together with 2 tablespoons of water and season to taste. Store in the refrigerator for up to 3–4 days.

Sun-Dried Tomato Juice

makes about 6 cups

7 ounces shallots

1½ heads of garlic

20 ripe tomatoes, cored

2 red bell peppers, seeded

4 ounces (about ½ cup) sun-dried tomatoes

1¼ cups basil leaves

¾ cup thyme leaves

¾ cup tarragon

¼ cup sugar

½ cup white wine vinegar

freshly ground salt and pepper

1 Peel and slice the shallots and garlic. Slice the fresh tomatoes and bell peppers.

2 Put all of these in a pan with the sun-dried tomatoes, herbs, sugar, vinegar, and 2 cups water. Season. Bring to a boil and simmer for 10 minutes.

3 Take from the heat, cover, and leave in a warm place for 12 hours.

4 Strain into a clean bowl through cheesecloth, allowing it to filter through without forcing. The juice can be bottled and refrigerated for 2–3 days.

Red Pepper Reduction

makes about 3 tablespoons

1 pound bright red bell peppers

2 tablespoons sugar

1½ tablespoons white wine vinegar

1 Process the seeded and chopped peppers with 3½ tablespoons water in a blender to a purée. Squeeze through cheesecloth or a fine sieve.

2 Stir in the sugar and vinegar. Put in a pan and boil until reduced to a syrup.

3 Allow to cool and chill. Bring to room temperature before serving.

dried fruit & vegetable slices

It takes a little practice to find the right timings for your oven.

for Dried Eggplant or Carrot Slices:

Using a mandoline slicer or very sharp knife, slice the eggplant or carrot as thinly as possible at an angle, to produce oval-shaped slices. Lightly grease 2 sheets of parchment paper with butter, then sprinkle with sea salt (this helps to draw out the moisture from the vegetable).

Place a sheet of parchment paper on a baking sheet and lay the vegetable slices on top. Cover with the second sheet of parchment paper (this will keep the slices flat). Put in the oven on the lowest possible setting for about 2 hours, until completely dried out and crisp.

for Dried Tomato Slices:

Slice the tomatoes across as thinly as possible and then follow the method for dried eggplant or carrot, leaving for about 4 hours.

for Dried Celery Root Slices:

Slice the celery root as thinly as possible. Heat a little olive oil in a frying pan and fry the celery root briefly on both sides. Drain. Salt the slices and lay them between 2 sheets of parchment paper on a baking sheet. Put in the oven on the lowest possible setting for about 3 hours, until dry and crisp.

Dried Limes

Slice your limes as thinly as possible. Arrange on a nonstick baking sheet, and dust with confectioners' sugar. Put in the oven at its lowest possible setting and leave for 2–3 hours until completely dried and crisp. You can also do this with slices of apple, orange, or lemon.

Orange Powder

Pare off the peel from 10 oranges, remove any attached pith, and blanch the peel for 1 minute in boiling water. Refresh in cold water, drain, and pat dry, then arrange on a nonstick baking sheet. Sprinkle with salt and a little confectioners' sugar, then dry in the oven on its lowest possible setting for 2–3 hours until crisp. Grind to a powder in a food processor and pass through a fine sieve. Store in an airtight jar until required.

Carrot Powder

Peel 6 large carrots, then grate them. Wrap the grated carrot in cheesecloth and squeeze out excess juice. Spread the carrot out on a baking sheet, sprinkle with salt, and dry in the oven at its lowest possible setting for 2–3 hours until crisp. Grind to a powder in a food processor and pass through a fine sieve. Store as above.

Cèpe Powder

Clean fresh cèpes (porcini) and roughly chop them. Season with salt, then place them on a baking sheet. Leave in the oven on the lowest possible setting for 3–4 hours until crisp. Grind to a powder in a food processor and pass through a fine sieve. Store as above. (If you can't find fresh cèpes, use shiitake.)

A Note about Seasoning

One of the most important things a chef learns is how to season food correctly. Sometimes when people cook at home and are disappointed with the bland taste of a dish, I think it is because they have not been bold enough with the seasoning. Cooking is all about proportion and balance, and the use of salt and pepper is the basis of that. However, most recipes simply say "add salt and pepper to taste," or "add a pinch of salt," referring to seasoning once, perhaps twice, when a chef will automatically season at many stages.

Throughout the recipes in this book I have tried to point out the correct times to

season. However, seasoning is something that will come naturally when you cook the same dishes often enough. You get a feel for bringing the flavors through; after all, the idea of seasoning is to enhance the natural flavors of the food, not to be the dominant taste.

When cooking meat or fish, I always salt it before cooking, otherwise as the meat or fish cooks it will become sealed on the outside, creating a wall against whatever seasoning you add to it, and preventing it from being absorbed properly into the flesh. With sauces, I season at the beginning of cooking, then taste and adjust as necessary at the end.

I use only unrefined coarse sea salt, because it brings out the flavors of food without adding an artificial saltiness. Before each service, it is crushed and placed in bowls, accessible to all the chefs. The pepper we use is a mixture of black and white peppercorns freshly crushed with a few coriander seeds in the food processor to give a fine pepper that won't leave sauces looking speckled.

Deep-Fried Herbs

When certain large-leaved herbs are deep-fried
in vegetable oil they take on an intense color
and translucence, like stained glass. Basil and
bay give the most stunning effects. The most
important thing is to dip the leaves only
briefly in the hot oil. As they are lowered in,
they will crackle as their moisture comes in
contact with the oil. The moment they stop
crackling, remove them with a slotted spoon
and drain them on paper towel.

Caramel Springs

As Marco Pierre White is fond of reminding me, in cooking you cannot reinvent the wheel. You can only try to find and perfect different ways of combining and presenting ingredients. Well, I didn't invent caramel, of course not, but one day, when I was in the kitchen at TV cook Keith Floyd's pub in Devon, England, I accidentally discovered a way of working with it that I believe to be original.

I was making some caramel cages (very fashionable at the time) and I left my spoon in the pot to do something else. When I came back, I found a tiny thread of caramel wound around the handle of the spoon: it looked like a perfectly coiled spring. It was set hard and when I slid it off the handle, it kept its shape.

My problem was to reproduce it. I tried using the handle of a wooden spoon, but if the atmosphere was humid, the caramel would cling to the wood, so I tried drying out the spoon in the oven before using it. That didn't help. I tried winding the caramel around pens and every kind of cylinder I could find in the kitchen. Finally, I tried a knife-sharpening steel, which gave me the perfect spring: the diameter was just right, and its coldness set the caramel the moment it touched it.

Working with caramel requires understanding and patience. Unless, like me, you have a restaurant full of customers demanding it, it is not something to work with when you are in a hurry or a bad mood. And it is easiest to make on a cool day, as heat and humidity can make it damp and sticky to handle.

Like a steam train, the caramel process starts slowly, but when it gets up speed you have to be careful not to let it run away from you or the caramel will burn. The way to control it is to keep it at a gentle, steady pace.

We make caramel by heating unrefined white sugar in a heavy-based pan (some people add corn syrup, or a little water). We always use unrefined sugar, as it has a purer taste. As you heat the sugar slowly, it will turn first to a transparent liquid, then begin to color and caramelize at about 300ºF. After that it will pass through a shade that is just darker than gold — take it from the heat quickly or it will color rapidly and when it reaches around 375ºF will burn and taste bitter.

Always take care when working with caramel; if you splash yourself with it, it will retain its heat after hitting your skin, causing a bad burn.

Make your springs just before you need them, then you have to be quick. Take a spoon in one hand and hold a sharpening steel in the other. Dip the spoon into the hot caramel, then lift it out, pulling a thin thread of caramel after it. Quickly wind this five or six times around the steel, pulling the thread very slightly as you do so, so that the spirals are about 3/4 inch apart. The caramel will set almost instantly and, as it does so, slide the spring carefully from the sharpening steel and place on a sheet of parchment paper folded up into a series of accordion folds until you need it.

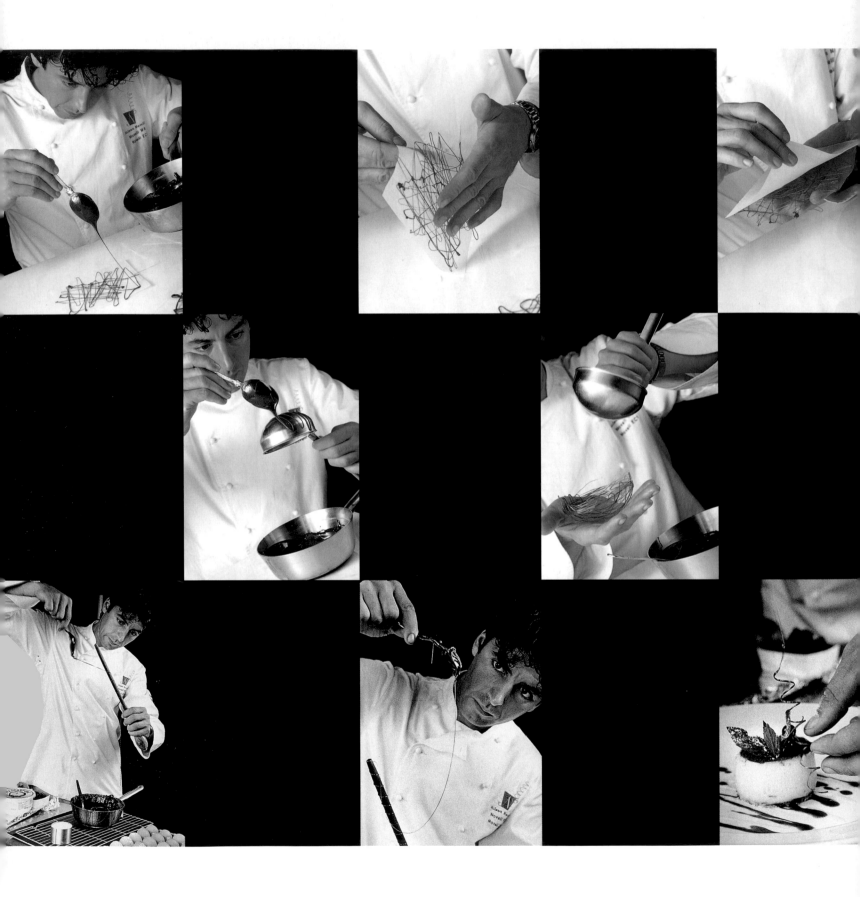

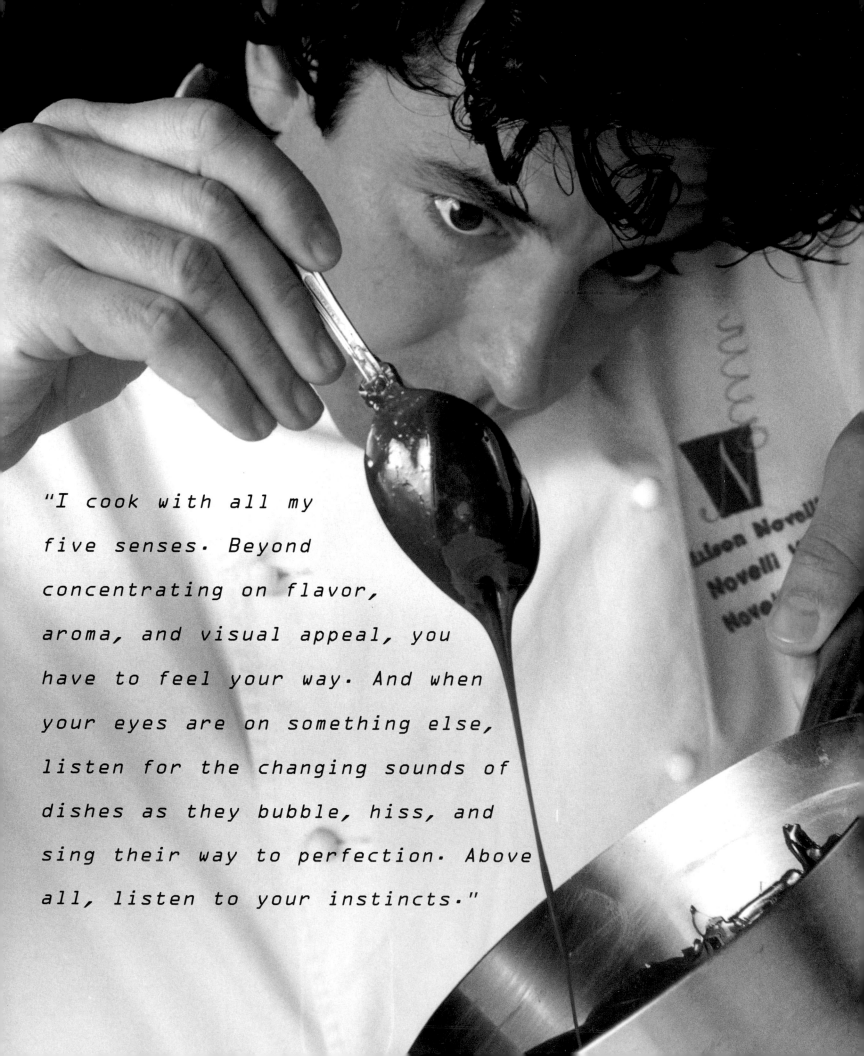

"I cook with all my five senses. Beyond concentrating on flavor, aroma, and visual appeal, you have to feel your way. And when your eyes are on something else, listen for the changing sounds of dishes as they bubble, hiss, and sing their way to perfection. Above all, listen to your instincts."

fish &

shellfish

When I see the fresh fish
arriving in the kitchens each morning,
I find myself imagining the parts of the world
it has come from. I can smell the sea on the
scales, and I feel the creativity starting to
flow. I get so much pleasure from cooking fish,
because it is so easy to create a special meal
by doing very little. I hate to see wonderful
fish played about with or smothered in rich
sauces. Freshness is always the key. Look for
bright, shiny fish with clear eyes and pink
gills, but also remember that a really fresh
fish has no smell, until you begin to cook
it. All you should smell is the sea. If a
fish is old, then it smells fishy and it
is fit only for the garbage. If a fish is
really fresh, you can even hear the crack
of freshness when you lift the gills,
like the stalk of a fresh flower
snapping. There are so many ways to
cook fish: all you need is the
confidence not to overcook it and
to let it speak for itself.

scallops

There is something very secretive and sensual about the scallop, a pearl of sweetness hiding inside a closed shell. It has an air of luxury about it, yet of all the shellfish it is probably the best value. It looks delicate, but has the flavor and texture to combine with a surprising number of ingredients. Sometimes I worry that one day there won't be enough scallops left in the sea to feed our insatiable demand for them, because I can't imagine cooking without them.

Always buy diver scallops, rather than dredged ones, which will have been dragged out of the sea at low tide, picking up grit as they go. This can give them a gray color, unlike the fresh, white, firm flesh of the diver scallop. Unless your market can assure you that they are diver scallops, try whenever possible to examine the scallops still in their shells. The shell of a dredged scallop will be broken up around the edges where it has been dragged. Diver shells will be intact, and normally still covered in barnacles. Also, beware of the practice of soaking scallops to plump them up. As soon as you cook them, this liquid will ooze out and the scallops will shrink.

The shells should always be closed, or will close if you tap them. If the shell stays open, the scallop is dead. Diver scallops are sorted and graded according to size by the divers. Buy the biggest sea scallops you can (up to about 3 inches) for pan-frying, because they are the sweetest. The smaller bay scallops require only the shortest cooking. I like to drop them briefly into a flavorful nage (a court-bouillon with cream; see the recipe on page 26), and serve them as canapés in the bar.

Should the scallops be sold with their corals (i.e. the roe), these should be bright orange, plump, and firm, not pale yellow and flat. The color is usually another sign of freshness. When we pan-fry scallops we remove any corals, as they have quite a strong flavor that can dominate a dish. However, we often use them in sauces, to impart their intense, fishy taste, or dry them and grind them to a powder for dusting fish.

Pan-Fried Scallops with Orange, Vanilla, and Cardamom

The perfect pan-fried scallop has a golden brown, slightly caramelized crust and a center that is just translucent. If the flesh is white and opaque all the way through, it will be dry and chewy.

To achieve that fabulous crust (and this applies to all fish and shellfish) it is important to get a well-seasoned or nonstick pan hot first, before you even add the oil, then get the oil very hot before you put in the scallops. If you add oil to a cold pan, you won't get the intensity of heat, and the moisture will leach out of the scallop into the oil, boiling — rather than searing — the flesh, and causing it to toughen up. The idea is to seal that moisture inside the scallop as quickly as possible, cooking for no more than a minute on each side.

This recipe demonstrates perfectly the way that scallops work with unusual flavors to create something special, yet very simple to prepare. In this case the combination of orange, vanilla, and cardamom perfectly complements the caramelized sweetness of the scallops.

serves 4

a little olive oil

freshly ground salt and black pepper

12 large sea scallops

3 ounces baby spinach leaves

¾ cup Orange, Vanilla, and Cardamom Infused Oil (page 11)

sprigs of sage, to garnish

1 Heat a frying pan until very hot, then add a thin film of olive oil. When this is also very hot, season the scallops, and pan-fry them for 1 minute on each side, until golden brown.

2 Arrange the spinach on 4 serving plates. Place the scallops on top. The heat from them will wilt the spinach.

3 Dribble some of the infused oil around each plate and garnish with the sage.

Glazed Scallops, Fava Beans, Orange, Vanilla, and Cardamom

From the simple idea of pan-fried scallops flavored with orange, vanilla, and cardamom, you can build up a more elaborate dish using the intense reduction of those flavors, rather than the oil, to add a "glaze" to the scallops, together with some fava beans and diced tomatoes. For the garnish you can make a feature of the vanilla beans.

serves 4

½ pound (about 1½ cups) shelled fresh fava
    beans
2 tomatoes
a little olive oil
freshly ground salt and pepper
8 large sea scallops
2 vanilla beans, split lengthwise
sprig of mint, chopped
Orange and Cardamom Reduction (page 11),
    seeds from ½ vanilla bean added while still
    warm

for the garnish:
4 large sprigs of chervil
garden cress

1 Blanch the beans briefly in boiling water, refresh under cold running water, and squeeze the bright green beans out of their skins.
2 Blanch the tomatoes briefly in boiling water, drop them into a bowl of cold water, then remove the skins. Quarter the tomatoes, scrape out the seeds, and dice the flesh into ¼-inch cubes.
3 Heat a pan until very hot, then add a little olive oil and heat until this is also very hot. Season the scallops and then sauté them for 1 minute on each side, until golden brown. A few seconds before you take them from the heat, toss in the fava beans, vanilla beans, tomatoes, and mint, and season again.
4 To serve: Arrange some fava beans and tomatoes in the center of each plate, with 2 scallops on top and a halved vanilla bean tilting upward between them. Dribble on some Orange and Cardamom Reduction, and garnish with chervil and garden cress.

Scallop Feuillantine

Once you feel comfortable pan-frying scallops, you can build up a more complicated dish like this favorite of mine which I have recently revamped.

serves 4

for the sauce:

a little olive oil

4 shallots, minced

4 mushrooms, minced

¼ cup minced fennel

1 garlic clove, minced

1 lemongrass stalk

2 cups dry white wine

2 cups fish stock, homemade or frozen, or
    2 cups bottled clam juice

⅔ cup heavy cream

freshly ground salt and pepper

8 baby fennel bulbs, or 2 slender fennel bulbs
    quartered lengthwise

2 tomatoes

2 large sheets of phyllo (at least 12 x 6 inches)

2 egg yolks, beaten

olive oil, for sautéing

12 large sea scallops, any corals reserved

1 lemongrass stalk, cut in 4 lengthwise

handful of chopped chives

chervil sprigs, to garnish

1 Preheat the oven to 350°F.

2 First, make the sauce: Heat the olive oil in a heavy-bottomed pan, add the minced vegetables and garlic, and sweat very gently, until the vegetables are translucent.

3 Heat a little more oil in another pan and sauté any scallop corals with the lemongrass for 2–3 minutes. Add to the vegetables.

4 Pour in the wine and reduce by about one-third, then add the stock and reduce again by two-thirds. Add the cream, season, and bring to a boil. Turn down the heat and simmer 5 minutes. Strain into a clean pan.

5 Meanwhile, blanch the fennel about 1 minute in boiling salted water. Drain, refresh under cold running water, and reserve.

6 Blanch the tomatoes briefly in boiling water, drop them into a bowl of cold water, then remove the skin. Quarter the tomatoes, scrape out the seeds, and dice the flesh into ¼-inch cubes. Reserve.

7 Lay out one sheet of phyllo pastry on a clean work surface and brush with the beaten egg. Place the second sheet of phyllo on top and brush with egg.

8 Leave the phyllo to dry for 3 minutes, then cut out 8 circles, about 3 inches in diameter.

9 Place these circles, egg-glazed side down, on a baking sheet lined with parchment paper. Cover with another sheet of parchment paper to prevent the pastry from rising, then bake for 3–4 minutes, until golden.

10 Heat a frying pan until very hot, then add a little olive oil, and heat until this is also very hot. Season the scallops and sauté them with the lemongrass for 1 minute on each side, until golden brown. As you turn them, put in the blanched fennel to heat through.

11 In a separate pan, heat a little olive oil, add the chopped tomato and chives, and heat these through. Warm the sauce through.

12 Place a scallop in the center of each plate. Top with a piece of fennel and a round of phyllo. Follow this with 2 scallops, a strip of lemongrass, another piece of fennel, and the second round of phyllo. Pour the sauce around. Garnish with the tomato and chive mixture and chervil sprigs.

"I can't conceive of my kitchen without scallops."

Bay Scallops with Artichoke Nage

In this recipe, the time is spent on preparing the *nage* (poaching liquid) and the scallops are added literally at the last moment. Served in scallop shells, they make wonderful canapés or appetizers.

serves 4

4 artichokes

equal quantities dry white wine and water, for cooking

4 shallots, minced

4 baby carrots, minced

8 asparagus spears

48 bay scallops, plus 4 large or 12 small shells for presentation

for the nage:

a little olive oil

4 shallots, minced

1 garlic clove, minced

1 celery stalk, minced

6 mushrooms, minced

1 bay leaf

sprig of thyme

1 cup dry white wine

½ cup fish stock, homemade or frozen, or ½ cup bottled clam juice

½ cup heavy cream

freshly ground salt and pepper

¼ cup chopped chives

8 basil leaves, chopped

for the garnish:

garden cress

basil leaves

a little caviar or lumpfish caviar

1 Prepare the artichokes: Remove the stalks and peel away all the outside leaves. Remove the chokes (the hairy cores), to leave the fleshy bottoms.

2 Simmer these in the white wine and water (enough to cover) for about 40 minutes, until tender. Drain, cut in wedges about the same size as the scallops, and reserve.

3 Prepare the rest of the vegetables: Blanch the shallots and carrots in boiling water for 1 minute, drain, and refresh under cold running water. Reserve.

4 Peel and blanch the asparagus in the same way. Cut off the tips and halve lengthwise. Slice the stalk thinly. Reserve.

5 To make the nage: Heat the olive oil in a pan and gently cook the shallots, garlic, celery, and mushrooms with the herbs over a low heat, until soft but not colored.

6 Add the white wine and simmer gently for about 30 minutes.

7 Add the fish stock and simmer for a further 20 minutes.

8 Add the cream and bring back to a simmer. Season to taste, then take off the heat and strain through a fine sieve.

9 Return the nage to the heat and add the reserved artichokes, shallots, carrots, and asparagus. Bring to a boil, then add the scallops, and immediately take the pan from the heat. Leave for 1 minute for the scallops to continue cooking, then stir in the chopped chives and basil.

10 Spoon into the scallop shells, reserving about 4 tablespoons of the liquid. Froth up this liquid with a hand blender and spoon a little froth over each shell. Garnish with garden cress, basil, and caviar or lumpfish caviar.

brochettes

When we have parties for guests at the restaurants, I like to serve brochettes of baby squid and langoustines interspersed with basil leaves and cherry tomatoes. The brochettes are also one of our best-loved first courses. Instead of skewers made from wood or metal I use stalks of lemongrass, which release their perfume and flavor into the seafood as the brochettes cook. It is a simple idea, but the result is delicious, and people love it.

Jumbo Shrimp and Lemongrass Brochettes

These scaled-down jumbo shrimp brochettes have the flavor of the restaurant version that follows, but take very little time.

makes 12

12 raw jumbo shrimp, peeled

4 lemongrass stalks

12 large basil leaves

12 cherry tomatoes

for the marinade:

olive oil to cover

10 basil leaves

10 sun-dried tomatoes, chopped

well ahead, ideally the day before:

1 Mix the marinade ingredients, add the shrimp, and leave to marinate in the refrigerator overnight, or throughout the day if you are serving the dish for dinner.

when ready to cook:

2 Peel the outer leaves from the lemongrass, until the stalks are thin and pointed, then cut each in thirds.

3 When ready to cook, preheat a hot broiler or barbecue. Remove the shrimp from the marinade and wrap each shrimp in a basil leaf. Thread a wrapped shrimp and a cherry tomato on each lemongrass "skewer."

4 Broil or grill the kebabs for about 1 minute on each side, basting with the marinade, until the shrimp are cooked.

Squid and Langoustine Lemongrass Brochettes

This more extravagant version can be served with salad leaves as a first course or even a light lunch. They can be cooked on the grill, or broiled, or pan-fried.

serves 4

12 raw langoustines or jumbo shrimp

freshly ground salt and pepper

12 prepared baby squid (calamari)

24 basil leaves

4 lemongrass stalks

20 cherry tomatoes

thyme leaves

for the marinade and sauce:

1 cup olive oil

2 teaspoons Basil Oil (page 11)

2¾ cups Sun-Dried Tomato Juice (page 12)

to serve:

4 ounces curly endive leaves

4 bunches of arugula

Sherry Dressing (page 11)

sprigs of chervil and dill, to garnish

when ready to cook:

8 Unless you are pan-frying the brochettes, preheat a hot broiler or barbecue.

9 To make the sauce: Put the remaining Sun-Dried Tomato Juice in a pan and boil until reduced to a syrup.

10 Remove the brochettes and tomatoes from the marinade. Grill, broil, or pan-fry over high heat on all sides until golden brown, basting and sprinkling on the thyme just before the end of cooking. Also grill, broil, or pan-fry the halved tomatoes briefly.

11 Combine the endive and arugula and toss with the Sherry Dressing.

12 To serve: Arrange some dressed greens in the center of each plate and place a brochette on top. Pour the sauce over and around the brochette, and garnish with the cherry tomato halves and some sprigs of chervil and dill.

well ahead, ideally the day before:

1 Peel the langoustines or jumbo shrimp, leaving the tail piece in place. Make an incision along the back and remove any dark veins of intestinal tract. Season.

2 Rinse the squid bodies and tentacles well; pat dry and season both.

3 Wrap the langoustines or shrimp in basil leaves, then place inside the baby squid bodies, leaving the tails sticking out.

4 Peel the outer leaves from the stalks of lemongrass, until the stalks are thin and pointed.

5 Using the sticks of lemongrass as skewers, thread each of them first through a cherry tomato, then through a filled baby squid body (crosswise), then through a basil leaf and some squid tentacles, a second filled baby squid body, another basil leaf and another set of squid tentacles. Repeat with a third filled squid, final basil leaf, and set of squid tentacles. Finish with a second tomato. Repeat this with the remaining lemongrass skewers. Reserve the remaining tomatoes.

6 To make the marinade: Mix together the olive oil, basil oil, and one-third of the sun-dried tomato juice. Halve the remaining tomatoes and add to the marinade.

7 Season the brochettes, then leave to marinate in this mixture in the refrigerator overnight or throughout the day.

cooking en papillote

The point of cooking fish *en papillote* (i.e. in a package of parchment paper) is to steam the fish in its own juices, then to open up the paper package on your plate, releasing all the wonderful aromas. When you make your package, which will look a little like a paper turnover, don't fold it up too tightly. It should be a little slack, so that the package can puff up with steam without the paper splitting.

Papillote cooking is most suited to small fillets of fish, because larger pieces would take too long to cook. The first recipe is for a simple red porgy *papillote*; the second is a more impressive restaurant variation, using mussels and coconut.

Red Porgy en Papillote with Lemongrass and Shallots

serves 4

4 red porgy fillets, each about 6–8 ounces, scaled and with pin bones removed
½ cup olive oil
freshly ground salt and pepper
6 shallots, thinly sliced
2 garlic cloves, chopped
4 lemongrass stalks, thinly sliced
a little egg white

1 Preheat the oven to 475°F. Coat the fish in olive oil and season.

2 Take 4 large squares of parchment paper about 12 x 12 inches. In the center of each sheet, arrange a bed of shallots, garlic, and lemongrass and season. Place a fillet on top.

3 Brush the edges of the paper with egg white and fold them over the top of the fish. Bring the edges together and pleat a series of folds to seal, so that you have a paper package resembling a turnover. Repeat until you have 4 packages.

4 Sprinkle a little water over each package, place on a baking sheet, and bake in the preheated oven for about 8 minutes, until the package puffs up and turns crisp and brown.

5 Put the packages on plates and cut open with scissors at the table.

mussels

I really love mussels cooked *en papillote* (see page 32), which is ironic because when I was very young I didn't like mussels at all. In the north of France, where I come from, *moules-frites* (mussels and french fries) are the equivalent of the English fish and chips. Everywhere you see trucks selling them to eat out of paper. We used to buy mussels instead of candy bars.

I always thought of mussels as the dish of the poor. We didn't have much money, like most of the families we knew, so we would have soup and bread, or crêpes, and often mussels. Then one day, when my mother gave me mussels, she said to me: "This might be the dish of the poor, but the more you eat, the more you have on your plate," meaning the pile of shells you accumulate — with artichokes it is similar. It seemed a very clever idea to me and I liked eating mussels after that.

I would spend hours walking on the beach, trying to find mussels clinging to the rocks. Fishing didn't interest me, but looking for mussels and crabs was like searching for treasure. Sometimes I used to take a little stove on my bicycle and cook my finds on the beach. The mussels I found were always small — then, of course, I realized it was because other people had been there before me and left the small ones behind, because the large plump ones taste the best.

I will let you in on the secret of how we make our mussels bigger. It might sound a little crazy, but it is a tip I learned from the local people in France. Remember, as long as the mussels are closed, they are alive and can feed. First clean the mussels, then put them in a bucket with enough water to cover and a couple of handfuls of oats. Mix everything around with your hands, then mix again every six hours or so, for two days. The mussels will eat the oats and grow bigger. Before cooking, if any of the shells open and won't close when tapped, throw them away. The mussels should all open in the steam of the *papillote*, just as they would if you were steaming them in a covered pan with wine and herbs for *moules marinières*.

Sometimes, for fun, we serve the following dish accompanied by a straw, so that you can drink the juices while you pick up the mussels in your fingers — the best way is to use one emptied mussel shell like a pair of tweezers to remove the rest.

When you put your *papillotes* on plates ready to serve, shake each plate gently, to disperse the liquid through the shells inside the packages before opening, so that the mussels are nice and moist. Be sure to discard any mussels that haven't opened.

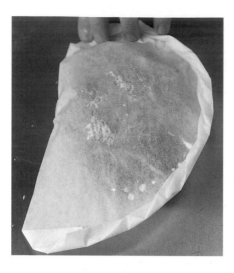

Mussel Papillote with Coconut Milk, Ginger, and Lemon Balm

This is a dish to please all the senses. When you open up the *papillote,* the color of the mussel shells and the aromas of coconut, ginger, and lemon balm are fantastic.

serves 4

3 pounds mussels

2-inch piece of fresh gingerroot, minced

12 lemon balm leaves

2 lemongrass stalks, sliced

juice and julienned peel of 1 lemon

juice and julienned peel of 1 lime

8 garlic cloves, thinly sliced

freshly ground salt and pepper

1 cup coconut milk

a little egg white

1 Preheat the oven to 475°F. Scrub off all dirt and beards from the mussels. Clean them in several changes of water, lifting out the mussels each time. Discard any that remain open.

2 Combine the ginger, lemon balm, lemongrass, lemon and lime peel and juices, and garlic in a bowl. Add the mussels, season, and mix well.

3 Take a large length of parchment paper, then spoon a quarter of the mixture into the center. (You might find it easier to press the paper into a shallow bowl, then spoon in the mussels; this stops them from rolling around.) Dribble over one-fourth of the coconut milk. Brush the edges of the paper with egg white. Taking care not to rip the paper, gather it up and seal the edges together. Then pleat a series of folds around the edge to form a package. Transfer to a baking sheet. Make 3 more packages.

4 Sprinkle a little water over each package and bake for about 10 minutes. When the paper is brown the mussels should be ready to eat.

5 Serve in the packages on plates, and remember not to eat any mussels that have failed to open.

trout tartare

For me this dish is one of the best examples of how you can take a simple idea and present it just as it is, or develop and embellish it until it becomes something special.

I first made the tartare at The Provence Restaurant in Lymington in Hampshire, England, where I got my first Michelin star. These were what I call my "crazy days," when I spent every minute of my time trying to come up with newer and more original shapes, colors, flavors, and textures for my dishes. If you will forgive me sounding sexist, I created this dish with women in mind, because we had many women lunching at the restaurant. It seemed to me that it was the sort of thing they wanted: light, fresh, and easy to eat.

From the simple tartare, a combination of sea trout (trout from the sea, rather than the river), asparagus, and cucumber bound by a piquant anchovy mayonnaise, I dressed it up with a pool of gazpacho sauce, based on the flavors of the Spanish soup, crowned it with wafer-thin slices of crisp cucumber, and topped that with a lightly boiled quail egg and a sprinkling of caviar. It has become one of my signature dishes.

Once I had made it the first time, the nightmare was to teach my team in the kitchen to do it quickly during service. I must have been a horror to work with, forever creating these dishes, then expecting my chefs to recreate them for fifty people. Like running a marathon, you do it over and over again, getting the time down on each occasion. The biggest job is the cucumber crown, as the cucumber has to be sliced at the last minute, so that it stays crisp. Now, any chef in my restaurants can put together the tartare in two and a half minutes.

Incidentally, the word "tartare" was used simply to refer to a kind of mayonnaise for serving with fish or a dish of seasoned raw ground steak (something that I really cannot understand anyone serving or wanting to eat). These days, by extension, it is often used for any dish in which the fish is chopped and served raw or marinated, rather than cooked. Unlike raw meat, however, the fish is cured in salt before being marinated, in this case for twenty-four hours before you want to serve it.

If you don't want to make gazpacho sauce or cucumber crowns, the tartare is a simple and satisfying first course without any extra elaboration, apart from some good bread. It also makes excellent canapés, spread on thin bite-sized pieces of bread. Alternatively, you could do as I do in my brasseries and garnish it just with an arrangement of salad leaves perched on top of the tartare.

Simple Trout Tartare

serves 4

1 pound skinless fillets of fresh sea trout
    or Arctic char
about ¾ cup sea or kosher salt

for the marinade:
2 cups olive oil
juice of 1 lime
large handful of chopped mixed herbs,
    such as basil, tarragon, lemon
    balm
1 head of garlic, halved

8 asparagus spears, trimmed
½ deep-green English cucumber, halved
    lengthwise

for the Anchovy
Mayonnaise:
2 egg yolks
1 tablespoon white wine vinegar
1 teaspoon grain mustard
5 anchovy fillets in oil, drained and
    coarsely chopped
5 basil leaves, chopped
1 cup olive oil
1 tablespoon hot water
freshly ground black pepper

to serve:
4 large sprigs of chervil
some good bread

the day before:
1 Cover the trout completely on both sides
with the sea salt. Chill for 1½ hours.

2 Rinse the salt from the trout, drain well, pat dry, and place in a bowl.

3 Mix together all the marinade ingredients in a separate bowl and pour over the trout. Cover and refrigerate overnight.

next day:

4 Cook the asparagus in boiling salted water until just tender, refresh in cold water, and drain. Then cut it into ¼-inch dice and reserve.

5 Dice the cucumber into pieces the same size as the asparagus.

6 Make the Anchovy Mayonnaise: Put all the ingredients except the olive oil and hot water in a blender or food processor and blend together. Add the olive oil, drop by drop, continuing to blend and gradually increasing the addition of the oil to a trickle, then add the hot water until you have a thick, smooth mayonnaise (it is important to add the oil slowly and steadily in this way, rather than all at once, otherwise you run the risk of the mixture curdling). Season with pepper to taste. Reserve.

just before serving, assemble the tartare:

7 Remove the trout from the marinade, cut it into ¼-inch cubes, and combine with the asparagus and cucumber in a bowl. Add the Anchovy Mayonnaise and season with pepper (the anchovies will probably make the mixture salty enough). Mix thoroughly.

8 To serve: Either pile the mixture into shallow bowls or plates or, for a neater presentation, place a 2½-inch-diameter pastry ring in the center of each bowl or plate and pack each ring with the trout mixture, pressing down as you do so. Neaten off the top, then carefully slide off the pastry rings. Garnish each serving of tartare with a sprig of chervil and serve with bread.

Trout Tartare with Cucumber Crown, Quail Egg, Caviar, and Chilled Gazpacho Dressing

One of the things I love about serving the tartare in this more elaborate way is that it combines different textures and temperatures, in a way that really wakes up the tastebuds. The contrast within the tartare of the slight crunchiness of asparagus and the softness of the trout is echoed in the garnish of crisp cucumber and softly boiled quail egg. Served to perfection, the gazpacho dressing should be chilled, the tartare slightly less chilled, and the egg just warm — not hot, or it will cause the tartare to melt and collapse.

serves 4

for the Gazpacho Dressing:
1 pound cherry tomatoes
1 garlic clove, chopped
1 tablespoon white wine vinegar
½ teaspoon sugar
½ teaspoon salt
squeeze of lemon juice
½ cup olive oil

Simple Trout Tartare (as above)

for the garnish:
4 quail eggs
½ English cucumber, chilled
mixed salad leaves and herbs
Sherry Dressing (page 11)
4 teaspoons caviar or lumpfish caviar
4 sprigs of chervil

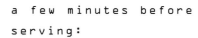

several hours ahead, make
the gazpacho dressing:

1 Blanch the tomatoes briefly in boiling water, drop them into a bowl of cold water, then remove the skin and seeds, and chop coarsely.

2 Using the same technique as for the Anchovy Mayonnaise (page 35), blend the tomato flesh and all the remaining ingredients except the olive oil in a blender. Then, with the motor still running, add the olive oil, drop by drop as before, then increasing the addition of the oil to a trickle until you have a smooth dressing. Pass through a fine sieve. Refrigerate until well chilled (at least 3 hours).

a few minutes before
serving:

3 Remove the tartare from the refrigerator to warm slightly.

4 Boil the quail eggs for about 1½–2 minutes, depending on their size, then remove from the pan and dip briefly into a bowl of ice water to halt the cooking process. As soon as the eggs are cool enough to handle, carefully peel off the shells.

5 Using the pastry rings as for Simple Trout Tartare, place a round of tartare in the center of each of 4 old-fashioned soup plates.

6 Slice the chilled cucumber in half lengthwise and scoop out the soft center. Slice each length very thinly into half-moon shapes, preferably using a mandoline slicer. Toss the mixed leaves and herbs with the Sherry Dressing.

7 Arrange the cucumber slices in an overlapping circle around the outside edge of the top of the tartare. Pile a bunch of mixed leaves and herbs in the middle of that, then nestle a quail egg in the center (fatter end downward), and garnish with a little caviar or lumpfish caviar. Decorate with sprigs of chervil.

8 Spoon the chilled Gazpacho Dressing around the base of the tartare and serve immediately — before the weight of the egg causes the tartare to sag!

cured & smoked salmon

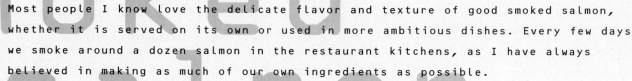

Most people I know love the delicate flavor and texture of good smoked salmon, whether it is served on its own or used in more ambitious dishes. Every few days we smoke around a dozen salmon in the restaurant kitchens, as I have always believed in making as much of our own ingredients as possible.

There are home smokers on the market, but you can also build one yourself, just as you would a barbecue grill. When I worked in various country restaurants I used to build my own smokers. I liked to start the smoking process early in the morning so that when guests arrived for lunch they could have a drink outside, with the wonderful aromas of the smoking salmon giving them an appetite.

I built my smokers with a brick surround, tall enough to install a grill about eighteen inches from the fire. Build your wood fire and let it die down to embers, then smother it with oak sawdust to suffocate the red glow. The oak will give a mellow character to the salmon. It is very important that when the fish goes on the grill there be no flame, only smoke; otherwise the salmon will cook. The smoker must be covered for at least three hours, so that the smoke envelops the fish; the flavor becomes stronger the longer it is smoked. The smoked salmon needs to be wrapped in plastic wrap to retain its smokiness. It can be eaten immediately, but if you let it get colder in the refrigerator, it is easier to slice.

Before smoking, the fish has to be cured and then marinated. If you are buying a whole salmon, don't choose one bigger than 10 pounds (when the head and bones are removed, you will be left with two fillets of about $3^1/4$ pounds each); otherwise the fillets will be too thick, making it difficult to cure them through to the center. Leave the skin on; it will make the fish easier to slice later.

The recipe on the next page is for a basic marinade. You can vary it by adding a little sesame or truffle oil, or even a syrup of lemongrass, in a ratio of about two-thirds syrup to one-third olive oil, giving a subtly different flavor to the salmon. To make the lemongrass syrup, first boil $1^1/4$ cups water with $1/2$ cup sugar, until the sugar dissolves, then simmer 10 broken-up lemongrass stalks in the syrup for 30 to 60 minutes. Remove from the heat and mix with the olive oil while still warm. Cool completely before use.

When you are planning to cure fish it must be absolutely fresh. For me, wild salmon is the best, because it has a beautiful natural color, and its firmer texture won't become flabby during the process. Firmness is another attribute that will help you to slice the salmon more easily. Always use coarse sea salt, rather than fine salt, because it will cure the fish without making it taste too salty.

Up to the point of smoking the fish, the curing and marinating process is the same as you would use to make gravadlax. If you want to do that, instead of smoking the salmon, roll it in a mixture of chopped dill and crushed peppercorns, then leave to cure in the refrigerator for 3 to 4 days. Serve sliced very thinly.

makes about 6 pounds

4 pounds coarse sea or kosher salt

2 tablespoons sugar

two 3-pound fillets of very fresh salmon

for the marinade:

olive oil

1 head of garlic, roughly chopped

handful of torn basil leaves, several sprigs of
    thyme, and bay leaves

10 shallots, sliced

ideally 2 days before:

1 Mix the salt and sugar. Place the fillets on a tray and completely cover both sides with this mixture. Cover with plastic wrap and leave in the refrigerator for about 4 hours.

2 To make the marinade: Heat a little olive oil in a pan and sweat the garlic, herbs, and shallots very, very gently until they are just soft, but not browned. Then add enough olive oil to cover, and heat gently to allow all the flavors to infuse. Cover and leave to cool, then chill until completely cold.

3 Rinse the salt mixture off the fish and pat dry. Put the cured salmon, skin side up, in the marinade (make sure it fully covers the fish), then leave, covered, in the refrigerator for at least 24 hours.

on the day you want to
smoke the fish:

4 Remove the salmon from the marinade and pat completely dry. (Make sure there is no excess oil, as it may flame if it drips on the ash and burn the fish.) Smoke according to the instructions that accompany your smoker, or to taste (see previous page).

5 Serve thinly sliced with lemon juice, accompanied by good bread.

Home-Smoked Salmon Salad with Spicy Eggplant Salsa, Poached Quail Egg, and Anchovy Dressing

Having smoked our own salmon, one of the ways we use it is in this simple salad.

serves 4

for the Eggplant Salsa:

3 tablespoons olive oil

salt and freshly ground black pepper

1 large eggplant, finely diced

6 shallots, minced

2 teaspoons sherry vinegar

1 tablespoon ground cumin

6 cardamom seeds

1 teaspoon garam masala

½ cup finely diced sour pickles

10 sprigs of cilantro, chopped

10 basil leaves, chopped

small bunch of chives, chopped

for the Anchovy Dressing:

1¼ cups olive oil

4 ounces anchovy fillets in oil, drained

2 tablespoons white wine vinegar

½ teaspoon chopped garlic

2 teaspoons water

4 quail eggs

8 slices of cured and smoked salmon

½ pound mixed salad leaves

fresh mixed herbs, to garnish

1 To make the Eggplant Salsa: Heat 2 tablespoons of the olive oil in a large pan, season the eggplant, and cook it slowly with the shallots, until the oil has been absorbed and the eggplant is soft.

2 Add the vinegar, spices, and pickles. Pour into a bowl and add the chopped herbs and the remaining oil. Cover with plastic wrap and leave until cool for the flavors to infuse. Adjust the seasoning if necessary.

3 To make the Anchovy Dressing: Put all the ingredients in a blender or food processor and process to mix. Season and reserve.

4 Poach the quail eggs (see opposite).

5 To assemble: Arrange the smoked salmon slices in the center of 4 plates and spoon some Eggplant Salsa around them. Toss the mixed salad leaves with the Anchovy Dressing, pile neatly in the center of the salmon, top with a quail egg, and garnish with the mixed herbs.

poached quail eggs

I like to use poached quail and chicken eggs as a garnish for salads. There is something delightful about the way a perfect soft, warm poached egg breaks into cold, crisp salad.

There is a saying in the restaurant trade that you can tell the caliber of a chef by the way he cooks eggs, and poaching is a very good test. This technique might sound a bit laborious, but I still think it is the best. In cooking, however, the simplest things are often the most difficult to achieve. You need to practice to find perfection.

In a busy restaurant kitchen we have to prepare poached eggs in advance of service, and it can make life easier at home, too, if you are preparing eggs for a number of guests. They can be kept in the refrigerator until you need them, when all you have to do is dip them in a pan of boiling water for 20 seconds — just long enough to heat the yolks without overcooking.

1 To a deep pan, add about 1 part white wine vinegar to 9 parts water. (Vinegar helps to coagulate the white of the egg, but be careful not to add too much or it will give a sour taste to the egg.) Don't salt the water, as the salt will counteract the effect of the vinegar. Bring the water to a steady simmer.

2 Grease a ladle with oil and the tiniest drop of white wine vinegar (this will begin to work on the egg white even before it goes into the water). Break your egg carefully into the ladle. The chef's way to do this is to hold the egg in one hand, tap it very gently against a sharp edge, then separate your thumb and fingers, in order to pull apart the shell (when I worked part-time at the local bakery as a schoolboy, there were so many eggs to crack that I used to do them two at a time, one in each hand).

3 Lower the ladle slowly into the water, letting

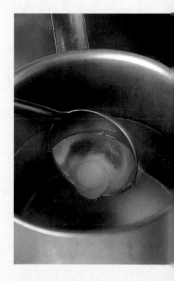

the water lap around it, so that the heat begins to set the white around the yolk. Don't let the water boil rapidly or it will disperse the white.

4 Let the ladle rest on the bottom of the pan briefly before turning the egg out. The egg will float upward, sending up a parachute of white. At this point you can skim off any scum that rises to the surface, so that you can see what is happening more clearly. It should take about 1½–2 minutes for the white of a quail egg to firm up, leaving the yolk still soft (allow about 2–2½ minutes for a chicken egg).

5 Lift the eggs out carefully with a slotted spoon. If you want chicken eggs to look their best, trim off any ragged edges of white with scissors. You really don't need to do this with quail eggs, as there is so little white. Transfer them into a bowl of ice water to stop them from cooking any further.

Glazed Cured Salmon and Beaufort Cheese Terrine

This quite extravagant dish is a way of using salmon that has been cured in salt and marinated as described on page 40, but not smoked — so it is a cousin of the marinated trout used for the tartare on page 35. Any substantial trimmings left over when the salmon is cut to fit the terrine could be used to make that dish, simply substituting the marinated salmon for the trout.

My inspiration for this dish came from the kind of combination of ingredients I like to see in a salad. A layer of pancetta surrounds the salmon, Ratte potatoes (small waxy salad potatoes), artichokes, and cheese, which are combined with garlic, thyme, eggs, and cream. When the terrine is sliced, pan-fried, and glazed, it takes on a smoky character that goes very well with the intense sweetness of the balsamic vinegar reduction.

makes one terrine of around 12 portions

1 pound Beaufort or Gruyère cheese, cut into
   ½-inch cubes

4½ cups dry Alsace or Riesling wine

1 fillet of salmon, about 3 pounds, cured and
   marinated as described on pages 39–40

20 thin slices of pancetta or bacon

2 tablepoons thyme leaves, picked and washed

4 garlic cloves, minced

freshly ground salt and pepper

20 Ratte (or other small waxy salad) potatoes,
   boiled and sliced

12 large cooked artichoke bottoms

2 cups heavy cream

3 whole eggs, plus 3 extra yolks

a little olive oil

for the Balsamic Reduction:

½ cup aged balsamic vinegar

3 tablespoons Madeira

3 tablespoons port

ideally two days before:

1 Put the cubed cheese in a bowl with the wine and leave to marinate overnight.

next day:

2 Preheat the oven to 300°F.

3 Trim the marinated salmon along its length and ends to make a rectangle of the right length to fit into a large terrine.

4 Line the terrine with 3 layers of plastic wrap, leaving an overhang of about 8 inches on each side to wrap over the top once filled.

5 Line the plastic wrap with strips of pancetta, again leaving an overhang all around to pull over the top of the terrine when filled.

6 Remove the cheese from the marinade with a slotted spoon and use half of it to make a layer on top of the pancetta. Sprinkle with a little thyme and garlic, and season (do this for every layer).

7 Follow with a layer of half the potato slices.

8 Lay 6 of the artichoke bottoms in a line down the center. Place the salmon fillet on top.

9 Continue the layers of cheese, potato, and artichoke as before, sprinkling each layer with thyme, garlic, and seasoning as you work.

10 Whisk the cream with the eggs and yolks until well combined. Season, then pour this mixture over the top.

11 Pull the overhanging pancetta neatly over the top to completely enclose the terrine.

12 Pull the overhanging layers of plastic wrap over the top, tucking into the opposite side with a spatula. Repeat all the way around.

13 Place the terrine in a larger baking dish and add hot water to come halfway up the sides of the terrine. Bake for 1–1½ hours, until just set. Allow to cool.

14 Cut a piece of thick cardboard to fit the top of the terrine. Press down gently, then wrap the entire thing as tightly as possible in plastic wrap, place something heavy on top, and refrigerate for about 12 hours.

to serve:

15 Make the Balsamic Reduction: Mix all the ingredients in a pan and simmer very slowly until reduced to a syrupy consistency.

16 Unmold the terrine and cut it into ¾-inch-thick slices.

17 Heat a little olive oil in a large frying pan and pan-fry the slices briefly over a high heat, until golden and glazed on each side and heated through to the center.

18 Unleash your artistic side with bold patterns of the Balsamic Reduction around the rim of each plate and place a slice of terrine on top.

Tuna Carpaccio

serves 4

1 pound very fresh tuna loin, trimmed
about ⅔ cup sea salt

for the marinade:
2 cups olive oil
handful of mixed rosemary, thyme, and basil
1 garlic clove, lightly crushed
pinch of whole black peppercorns
juice of ½ lemon

to dress and garnish:
½ cup each light and dark soy sauce
a little vegetable oil
1 shallot, thinly sliced
1 thin slice of gingerroot, minced

1 garlic clove, minced
scant ⅓ cup Asian sesame oil
5 ounces bean sprouts
a little chopped cilantro and basil
4 sprigs of chervil

the day before:
1 Put the tuna on a plate and cover on both sides with sea salt. Chill for 2 hours.
2 Rinse the salt from the fish, pat dry, and place in a bowl. Mix all the marinade ingredients and pour over the tuna. Chill overnight.

next day:
3 Remove the tuna from the marinade, pat dry, and wrap tightly in plastic wrap. Chill for about 4 hours until firm.

4 To make the dressing, put the soy sauces in a pan and reduce by two-thirds. In a separate pan, heat the vegetable oil and gently sweat the shallots, ginger, and garlic until softened but not browned. Add to the soy sauce. Leave to cool, then whisk in the sesame oil.
5 Cut the tuna across into about 20 slices.
6 Heat some more vegetable oil in a pan and stir-fry the bean sprouts quickly to heat through. Add the chopped cilantro and basil, season, and stir in a little of the dressing.
7 Arrange the tuna slices with one in the center of the plate and the rest overlapping around the outside. Season with pepper. Top with a spoonful of bean sprouts and dribble the rest of the dressing around. Garnish with chervil.

Mackerel Escabèche

For *escabèche*, fish is marinated in oil, vinegar, and herbs. Usually it is cooked first, but in this dish we marinate and *then* roast the mackerel.

serves 4

for the escabèche:
1 teaspoon coriander seeds
4 cardamom pods
4 shallots, thinly sliced
3 carrots, thinly sliced
1 red and 1 yellow bell pepper, peeled, seeded, and thinly sliced
1 slender fennel bulb, quartered and thinly sliced
1 teaspoon fine julienne of lemon peel
1 teaspoon fine julienne of orange peel, plus the juice of ½ orange
3 tablespoons white wine vinegar
3 tablespoons olive oil
1 teaspoon chopped cilantro
pinch of saffron

4 large mackerel fillets, all bones removed
handful of chopped cilantro

for the garnish:
Dried Carrot Slices (page 15)
a few sprigs of chervil

the day before:
1 First, make the escabèche: Crush the coriander seeds and cardamom pods lightly with a rolling pin, then put these and the rest of the escabèche ingredients in a pan. Cover and cook gently for 5–10 minutes, until the vegetables are cooked and soft. Remove from the heat, transfer to a bowl, and leave to cool.
2 Score the flesh of each mackerel fillet through the skin widthwise along its length, then roll up and secure with toothpicks. Put the fish into the escabèche mixture, turn to coat, cover and leave in the refrigerator overnight, turning from time to time when you can.

next day:
3 Preheat the oven to 425°F. Remove the fish from the escabèche mixture, reserving the mixture.
4 Heat an ovenproof frying pan. When it is hot, put in the fish and sear quickly on both sides.
5 Add 2 tablespoons of the escabèche liquid and the chopped cilantro, then transfer to the oven to cook for 4 minutes. Add the vegetables from the escabèche for the last minute.
6 To serve: Make a little mound of the vegetables on each of 4 plates. Remove the toothpicks from the fish fillets and place them on top. Pour the remaining pan juices over the top. Garnish each plate with Dried Carrot Slices and some chervil.

finnan haddie

I really love finnan haddie. I was first introduced to the combination of smoked haddock and eggs when I had to take my turn preparing the breakfasts at a country house hotel. Later I began to think of ways of presenting these two ingredients on lunch and dinner menus.

The first recipe is a simple assembly with puff pastry and hollandaise sauce. If you want to be a bit more adventurous, you can make the haddock into a *brandade*, which can be served with good bread, or as a filling for a baked potato, topped with a poached egg. To take this idea a stage further, we serve the *brandade* inside a baby pumpkin. We always try to use ingredients that are as natural as possible. Undyed smoked haddock usually indicates a higher quality of fish than the garish, yellow-dyed variety.

Smoked Haddock with Poached Egg and Puff Pastry

When we make our hollandaise sauce, we use clarified butter, as this helps to prevent separation.

serves 4

for the Hollandaise Sauce:
½ cup (1 stick) butter
2 egg yolks
1 tablespoon white wine
1 teaspoon white wine vinegar
1 tablespoon water
freshly ground salt and pepper

1 sheet of frozen puff pastry, thawed
1 egg yolk, beaten
2 fillets of undyed smoked haddock or other smoked
    white fish, each about 6 ounces
1¼ cups milk
2 tablespoons butter
4 eggs
3 bunches of watercress, stalks removed
a little Sherry Dressing (page 11)

for the garnish:
garden cress

1 Preheat the oven to 425°F.

2 Clarify the butter for the Hollandaise Sauce by heating it over a very low heat without stirring. Skim the foam from the surface, then remove the pan from the heat, and leave to stand for a few minutes. The white milk solids will sink to the bottom, allowing you gently to pour off the yellow clarified butter from the top. Reserve this and discard the white solids.

3 To make the Hollandaise Sauce: Place all the ingredients except the butter in a round-bottomed bowl and place this over a pan of simmering water. Whisk in a figure-eight motion as fast as possible until the sauce becomes as thick as whipped cream, then remove the bowl from the heat and slowly whisk in the clarified butter. If the sauce thickens too much, adjust it by whisking in a spoonful of hot water. Season the sauce to taste, and keep warm. Do not allow to boil at any time or the sauce will separate.

4 Roll out the puff pastry to a thickness of about ⅛ inch and cut 4 shapes of your choice. With the tip of a knife, score the top in diamond shapes, brush with the egg yolk,

and bake in the preheated oven for about 5 minutes until puffed up and golden. Reserve.

5 Use tweezers to remove the pin bones from the fish fillets and cut them to produce 4 equal portions.

6 Place the fish in a deep baking pan with the milk and butter and bake for about 8–10 minutes (or until the skin comes away easily).

7 Poach the eggs as described on page 41.

8 To assemble: Halve each puff pastry shape horizontally, to create a base and lid. Place a puff pastry base in the center of each plate. Dress the watercress with Sherry Dressing and place a small mound on top of the puff pastry base. Strip the skin from each fish fillet and place one on top of each watercress mound. Top with a poached egg and spoon some Hollandaise Sauce over the top. Finish with a lid of puff pastry and garnish with garden cress.

Smoked Haddock Brandade

If you like, you can bake two large potatoes in the oven, rather than boiling them.

Brandade is good with bread and salad, or some roasted bell peppers.

serves 4

3 large potatoes

3 pounds undyed smoked haddock or
    other smoked white fish fillets

2 garlic cloves, coarsely chopped

2 sprigs of thyme

about 2¾ cups milk

10 basil leaves, chopped

freshly ground salt and pepper

good bread, to serve

1 Cook the potatoes in boiling salted water until tender. Drain and mash.

2 Poach the haddock with the garlic and thyme in enough milk to cover, until the fish is cooked and flakes away from the skin. Drain, reserving the milk.

3 Remove the skin from the haddock and mash the flesh with the garlic and thyme. Mix in the potato and basil. Season to taste (go easy on the salt, as the haddock may be quite salty). If the mixture is too dry, add a little of the reserved milk.

4 Serve with slices of good bread.

Steamed Pumpkin and Smoked Haddock Brandade with Poached Egg and Baby Vegetables

serves 4

4 baby pumpkins

assorted baby vegetables, such as corn, carrots,
    zucchini, fennel, to serve

Smoked Haddock Brandade (see above)

4 eggs

a little butter

freshly ground salt and pepper

1 In a large pot, steam the pumpkins over boiling water until the skin is soft enough for the point of a knife to go through easily.

2 Meanwhile, cook the baby vegetables in boiling salted water until just tender, drain, and reserve.

3 Slice the tops off the pumpkins and reserve, remove the seeds, and scoop out the flesh. Mix the pumpkin flesh with the brandade and spoon back into the pumpkins.

4 Poach the eggs (see page 41) and place one on top of each pumpkin. Replace the tops.

5 Heat the butter in a pan and toss the baby vegetables in it to heat through. Season and arrange around the pumpkin.

broiled sole

We tend to pan-fry, rather than broil, because this is easier to control in a busy kitchen situation. At home, however, broiling is an excellent way to treat a slim fish such as sole. Always broil fish under a moderate heat on a broiler pan that is about 3 inches from the heat source (or 5 to 6 inches from the heat if you cannot control the broiler setting). Put it higher and the fish will burn, lower and the fish will boil in its own juices.

Broiled Lemon Sole on the Bone with Bibb Lettuce and Ginger Sauce

This is one of the quick and simple dishes we serve in the brasseries.

serves 4

½ cup shelled fresh fava beans

2 tomatoes

4 whole lemon sole or yellowtail
   flounders, each about 1 pound

a little olive oil

4 shallots, minced

1 teaspoon ground ginger

1 teaspoon minced fresh gingerroot

½ cup dry white wine

½ cup (1 stick) and 2 tablespoons
   unsalted butter

freshly ground salt and pepper

1 head Bibb lettuce, thinly shredded

handful of chives, chopped

squeeze of lemon juice

for the garnish:
mixed herbs
garden cress

1 Preheat the broiler. Blanch the fava beans in boiling water for 1 minute, drain, and refresh under cold water. Reserve.

2 Blanch the tomatoes briefly in boiling water, drop into a bowl of cold water, then remove the skin. Quarter the tomatoes, scrape out the seeds, and dice the flesh into $1/4$-inch cubes. Reserve.

3 Broil the fish, skin side uppermost first, for about 3 minutes on each side until just cooked through.

4 Heat the olive oil in a pan and sweat the shallots with the ground and fresh ginger until soft but not colored.

5 Add the white wine and simmer until almost all the liquid has evaporated.

6 Remove the pan from the heat and whisk in the butter. Season.

7 Just before serving, add the beans, lettuce, tomatoes, and chives to the sauce. Squeeze in some lemon juice.

8 To serve: Place a fish on each plate, pour the sauce over and around, and garnish with herbs and garden cress.

*"These colors,
these flavors,
speak to me of the
Mediterranean."*

Andalouse of Sole

This is a much more dramatic way to serve any type of sole.

serves 4

4 large sweet tomatoes

a little olive oil

2 garlic cloves, chopped

handful of chopped thyme

4 medium tomatoes

4½ cups Sun-Dried Tomato Juice
(page 12)

4 Dover sole or firm flounder fillets,
each about 7 ounces, halved

freshly ground salt and pepper

¾ cup black olives

4 chunks of Eggplant Caviar
(page 116)

10 basil leaves, chopped

1 teaspoon Red Pepper Reduction
(page 12)

for the garnish:

8 slices of Dried Eggplant
(page 15)

a little olive oil

more Red Pepper Reduction
(page 12)

well ahead, ideally the day before:

1 Blanch the large tomatoes briefly in boiling water and drop into a bowl of cold water. Remove the skins, then cut in half across their middles, leaving any attached stem in place, and scoop out the seeds. Put on a baking sheet, sprinkle with olive oil, half the garlic, and the thyme, and leave in the oven at its lowest setting, until

not quite dried but taking on the character of sun-dried tomatoes, 4–5 hours. Reserve.

about 20 minutes before serving:

2 Blanch and skin the rest of the tomatoes and cut into quarters. Remove the seeds, and dice the flesh into ¼-inch cubes. Reserve.

3 Preheat the broiler. Reduce the Sun-Dried Tomato Juice to a syrup in a pan. Keep warm.

4 Brush the fish fillets with a little olive oil and season. Broil about 2–3 minutes on each side, skin side upward first. If quite thick, they may need 4 minutes on each side.

5 Put the diced tomatoes, olives, Eggplant Caviar, and remaining garlic in a pan with the basil, roasted tomatoes, and Red Pepper Reduction to heat through. Season.

6 To serve: Pick out the chunks of Eggplant Caviar and place one in the center of each plate. Place the bottom half of a roasted tomato on top and fill with the olive and tomato mixture. Crisscross 2 halves of fish fillet on top. Follow with 2 slices of Dried Eggplant, brushing both tomato and eggplant with olive oil to give them a sheen. Place the top half of the tomato on top. Spoon some Red Pepper Reduction around.

poached turbot

There is nothing more beautiful than a piece of poached turbot. If you fry or roast it, it becomes tough, whereas if you poach it, it stays tender and moist.

The secret of poaching is doing it very, very gently, with the bubbles barely breaking the surface of the liquid, so that the fish stays intact.

Turbot Poached in a Fragrant Nage

The *nage* (poaching liquid) may be used immediately or kept in a sealed container in the refrigerator for 2 or 3 days. Serve the turbot simply, with some puréed potatoes or vegetables.

serves 4

for the nage:

a little olive oil

4 shallots, coarsely chopped

4 small carrots, coarsely chopped

1 celery stalk, coarsely chopped

2 garlic cloves, chopped

5 lemon balm leaves

1 bay leaf

1 sprig of thyme

1 tablespoon coriander seeds

1 tablespoon white peppercorns

1 star anise

peel of 1 lemon

1 cup white wine

freshly ground salt and pepper

4 thick fillets of turbot or halibut, each about
7 ounces

1 First make the nage: Heat the oil in a large heavy-bottomed pan and sweat the vegetables, garlic, herbs, spices, and lemon peel in it gently until the vegetables are soft but not colored.

2 Add $1\frac{1}{4}$ cups water and the wine. Season and simmer for 5 minutes, then remove from the heat, and leave to infuse for about 20 minutes.

3 Put the nage back on the heat and bring to a simmer. Put in the fish, cover and simmer for 8 minutes.

4 Remove from the heat and leave the fish to rest in the nage for 2 minutes. Remove the fish from the nage and keep warm.

5 Pass the nage through a fine sieve and reheat, if necessary. Serve with the fish.

Poached Turbot with Spinach, Almond Cauliflower Purée, and Coconut Sauce

I first made this dish at London's The Four Seasons, where we had a lot of Asian customers. Previously I used to do a velouté of turbot, then I tried the dish using coconut milk — and it worked perfectly. Turbot is a relatively bland fish that soaks up such flavors very well.

serves 4

for the Cauliflower Purée:

½ pound waxy potatoes, peeled and coarsely chopped (about 1½ cups)

½ pound cauliflower, coarsely chopped (about 2 cups)

1 garlic clove, chopped

about 2¾ cups milk

freshly ground salt and pepper

2 tablespoons butter

1 drop of almond extract

4 thick fillets of turbot or halibut, each about 7 ounces

for the poaching liquid:

1 large can of coconut milk (about 1¾ cups)

juice of ½ lime

2 tablespoons white wine

4 shallots, chopped

1 tablespoon chopped fresh gingerroot

1 tablespoon chopped lemongrass

1 tablespoon coriander seeds, crushed

10 cilantro leaves

3 lime leaves

freshly ground salt and pepper

for the garnish:

2 large tomatoes

a little olive oil

4 ounces baby spinach

handful of chopped chives

1 tablespoon Carrot Powder (page 15)

mixed herbs

4 slices of Dried Lime (page 15)

1 First make the Cauliflower Purée: Put the potato and cauliflower in a pan with the garlic and enough milk to cover. Season. Simmer until the vegetables are very soft to the touch, then drain off three-quarters of the milk.

2 Add the butter and almond extract, and process in a blender until smooth. Season again to taste and keep warm.

3 To cook the fish: Mix together all the ingredients for the poaching liquid and simmer the mixture, without allowing it to boil, for 10 minutes. Remove from the heat and leave for about 20 minutes to infuse.

4 Bring the liquid back to simmering point and put in the fish. Simmer for 8 minutes, then remove from the heat, and leave to rest for 2 minutes in the liquid.

5 Remove the fish and keep warm. Pass the liquid through a fine sieve into another pan and warm through.

6 Meanwhile, prepare the garnish: First make tomato concassé by blanching the tomatoes briefly in boiling water, then dropping them in a bowl of cold water, and removing the skin. Quarter, scrape out the seeds, and cut the flesh into $1/4$-inch dice.

7 Heat the olive oil in a pan, toss in the tomato concassé, and heat through. Season.

8 Place the baby spinach in a warm stainless-steel bowl with a little olive oil and chopped chives. Season and stir with your hand to wilt the spinach.

9 Froth up the reserved poaching liquid with a hand blender or whisk.

10 To serve: Pile a little spinach in the center of each plate and spoon some Cauliflower Purée on top. Place a piece of fish on top of the purée and decorate with the warm tomato concassé. Spoon the frothy sauce around the fish. Lightly dust with Carrot Powder and top with herbs and a slice of Dried Lime.

"This dish plays with Asian flavors and a classic concept. I add almond to the cauliflower purée, which complements the flavor of the coconut."

When chefs talk about "roasting" fish, what they mean is starting off the cooking process by searing it in a frying pan over a very high heat and then finishing it in the oven. For me, this is the best way to cook thick fillets of fish such as sea bass. The idea is to get a golden crust on the outside, which will seal the soft, moist flesh inside. If you were to poach sea bass it would become rubbery.

You need a metal-handled, nonstick frying pan that will transfer to the oven. As when cooking scallops, get it good and hot before adding the oil, and then make sure the oil is really hot before you put in the fish, so that it will sear immediately. Always sear the fish on the skin side first, very briefly, then flip the fish over and sear briefly again. Transfer it to a hot oven (425ºF), skin side down, to cook for 6—8 minutes. Because the skin is in contact with the pan, it will crisp up and protect the flesh from the heat.

It is always difficult to be precise about how long to cook a piece of fish, because it depends on its size and thickness. You can test it by inserting a toothpick into the center of the fish. It is ready when the toothpick comes straight out, without any pulling or sticking. The fish will carry on cooking for a little longer after it comes out of the oven, and by the time it is on the plate, it will be perfectly done. If you worry too much that the center of the fish is not quite cooked and then put it back into the oven, by the time it arrives on the plate it will be overcooked.

Roasted Sea Bass with Basil and Chorizo

I love chorizo, and one day I had the idea to cook it in oil, then use this oil for pan-frying bass. As the skin of the bass crisped up I discovered that it took on an unbelievable flavor. From here it was only a simple step to cooking the fish and chorizo together. Mixing fish and meat is something I love to do, when the ingredients marry together as well as these. You can serve the combination quite simply, or build on the flavors to make the elaborate version we serve in the restaurant (see page 58).

serves 4

a little olive oil

4 bay leaves

2 ounces Spanish chorizo sausage, thinly sliced

4 fillets of sea bass, each about 7 ounces

a few basil leaves

1 Preheat the oven to 425°F.

2 Get a large ovenproof pan very hot on the stove, then add the olive oil. When that is hot, add the bay leaves, chorizo, and the fish (skin side down), and briefly pan-fry. Flip over and cook the other sides briefly.

3 Turn the fish over again, so that it is skin side down, and transfer the pan to the oven to cook for about 5 minutes, or until the skin is golden and the flesh just cooked.

4 Served garnished with basil leaves.

sage beignets

These little deep-fried sage leaf packages stuffed with olive paste make an attractive and unusual garnish — particularly with fish dishes. To make 16 sage beignets: Wash 32 sage leaves and pat dry. Make some olive paste by processing 4 tablespoons pitted black olives with 1 garlic clove and moistening the mixture with a little olive oil. Season. Spread half the sage leaves with the paste and top each one with an anchovy fillet. Press another sage leaf on top of each to make a sandwich. Mix 1 tablespoon baking powder with 1 tablespoon cornstarch and 2 tablespoons all-purpose flour, and add just enough cold water to make a batter with the consistency of light cream. Coat each pair of stuffed sage leaves in batter and deep-fry in hot vegetable oil for 30–60 seconds, until puffed up and golden. Drain well on paper towel.

"Sea bass and chorizo – so sexy together."

Roasted Fillet of Sea Bass with Chorizo Oil, Eggplant Caviar, Basil, and Fennel

Here, the addition of two of my favorite flavors — sun-dried tomato and eggplant — turns the sea bass and chorizo into something extra-special. You could also try substituting merguez or any other hot spicy sausage for the chorizo.

serves 4

4½ cups Sun-Dried Tomato Juice (page 12)

8 baby fennel bulbs, or 2 slender fennel bulbs
    quartered lengthwise

a little olive oil

4 bay leaves

4 fillets of sea bass, each about 7 ounces

Eggplant Caviar (page 116)

2 ounces Spanish chorizo sausage, sliced

3 tablespoons black olives, halved

freshly ground salt and pepper

¼ cup blanched, skinned, seeded,
    and diced tomatoes (see page 24)

8 cherry tomatoes

1 sprig of basil, separated into leaves

1 tablespoon unsalted butter

for the garnish:

4 tablespoons Chorizo Oil (page 11)

Deep-Fried Basil Leaves (page 16)

4 Dried Tomato Slices (page 15)

1 Preheat the oven to 425°F. Put the Sun-Dried Tomato Juice in a pan and cook until reduced to a syrup. Reserve.

2 Cook the fennel in boiling water for about 3 minutes until *al dente*. Drain and keep warm.

3 On the stove, get a large ovenproof sauté pan very hot, then add the olive oil. When that is very hot, add the bay leaves and fry the sea bass briefly, skin side down. Flip the fish over and cook briefly.

4 Add the Eggplant Caviar (discarding the skin), cooked fennel, chorizo, and halved olives. Season. Turn the fish over again, so that the skin side is down, and transfer to the oven to cook for about 5 minutes, or until the skin of the fish is golden and the flesh just cooked.

5 Just before serving, add the chopped and whole cherry tomatoes to the pan along with the basil, and adjust the seasoning if necessary.

6 Heat the tomato syrup gently in a pan and stir in the butter. Season to taste.

7 To serve: Arrange the chorizo, fennel, olives, and chopped tomatoes in the center of each plate. Place a fillet of sea bass on top, together with a fried bay leaf. Pour some tomato syrup around, sprinkle with Chorizo Oil, and garnish with Deep-Fried Basil Leaves, cherry tomatoes, and a Dried Tomato Slice.

Confit of
duck or rabbit, roast
squab, cassoulet — these are
flavors that excite me and that I have
known since I was a child, but one of the reasons
I left France was that I knew it would be easier
for me to try something different with them away
from the classical French system of cooking. For
me, the idea of turning a cassoulet into a
marbled terrine or serving venison with
scallops in a spicy sauce is an adventure.

Of course, that doesn't mean you can't
enjoy a simply roasted quail or squab, but
you could also roast some more quail to
make an elegant quail ravioli for later,
or serve your squab with a tarte
Tatin of red onion.

It saddens me that so many people
have a game bird or a piece of venison
languishing in their freezer because
they simply don't know what to do
with it. I hope this chapter will
give you some ideas.

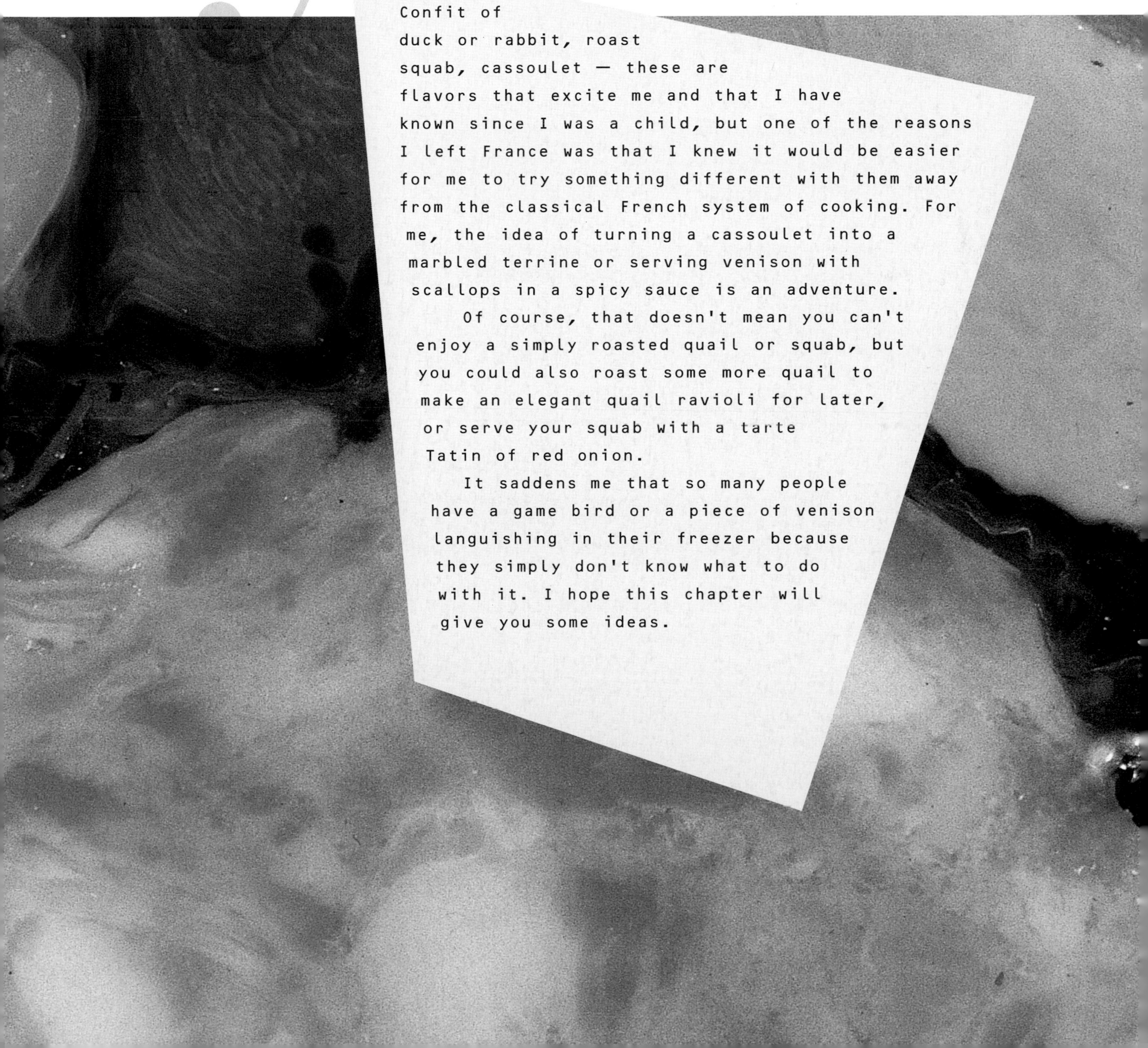

quail & chicken

Unlike chicken, which are more forgiving, quail are precious little birds that you must be careful not to overcook. The very best way of cooking them is to spit-roast them, so they brown evenly all round. Of course, you can also seal them all over in oil in a pan, then transfer the birds to the oven, as in the recipe opposite. It could also be used for poussin, or for chicken — though you would need to increase the roasting time to 12 minutes for a poussin, or 15 minutes per pound, plus 15 minutes, for a chicken.

Roast Quail with Broiled Pancetta

Instead of broiling the pancetta separately, which we do purely for garnish, you could use a little more and wrap it around the quail before cooking.

serves 4

olive oil

freshly ground salt and pepper

4 oven-ready quail

4 garlic cloves, unpeeled

4 sprigs of summer savory

4 bay leaves

8 thin slices of pancetta (Italian bacon) or
   bacon

12 peeled white grapes

1 Preheat the oven to 400°F.

2 Heat a little olive oil in a large ovenproof sauté pan. Season the quail and brown them all over in the oil.

3 Crush the garlic cloves gently to release their flavor, then add them to the pan with the savory and bay leaves. Roast in the oven for 6–8 minutes, until the juices run clear when the thickest parts of the birds' thighs are pierced.

4 Just before the end of cooking time, broil the pancetta until crispy, and add the grapes to the pan with the quail to heat through.

5 To serve: Put the quail in warmed serving dishes. Cross 2 slices of pancetta on top of each quail and garnish with roasted savory and bay leaves from the pan. Spoon the pan juices around.

Ravioli of Seared Quail and Foie Gras with Baby Leeks

Simply roasted quail is delicious as it is, but you can transform it into something more eye-catching by removing the breasts and legs and wrapping the breasts in fresh pasta to make a raviolo. This was just one element of the elaborate game plate I used to serve at London's Four Seasons, which also included Pigeon Tarte Tatin, Rabbit Cutlets and Venison with Truffle Mousse. However, it makes a great first course just on its own.

serves 4

4 roasted quail (see pages 62–3), herbs and
    pan juices reserved

4 sheets of fresh pasta (at least 8 inch square)

8 large basil leaves

freshly ground salt and pepper

½ pound canned, cooked foie gras, sliced into
    4 pieces

1 egg, beaten

½ cup veal demi-glace or 1 cup low-salt veal
    or chicken stock reduced over high heat
    to ½ cup

a little olive oil

for the leeks:

1 tablespoon chicken stock

1 tablespoon butter

2 tablespoons heavy cream

12 baby leeks

for the garnish:

4 tomatoes, blanched, skinned, seeded, and
    diced (see page 24)

a few chive stalks, finely snipped

chervil sprigs

1 Carefully remove the breasts and legs from the quail
and leave to cool.

2 Place the pasta on a floured board. From each sheet cut
a circle about 4½ inches in diameter and another about 3
inches in diameter.

3 Place a basil leaf in the center of each of the larger pasta
circles. Lay a quail breast half on top and season. Follow
this with a slice of foie gras, season again, then top with the
second quail breast half. Finish with another basil leaf.

4 Place the smaller circles of pasta on top. Brush the edges
of each pasta circle with a little beaten egg, then pinch the
two together to enclose the quail and foie gras. The ravioli
will resemble little double-crust pies in shape.

5 To cook the leeks: Put the chicken stock, butter, and
cream in a small pan and bring to a simmer. Add the leeks
and simmer for about 4 minutes, until the liquid has
thickened and coated the leeks, which should be tender.
Keep warm.

6 To make the sauce: Simmer the pan juices from cooking
the quail, add the demi-glace or reduced stock and bring
back to a simmer. Continue to bubble until thickened to a
saucelike consistency, then pass through a fine sieve, and
season to taste. Add the quail legs and keep warm.

7 To cook the ravioli: Bring a large pan of salted water to a
boil, add a drop of olive oil, and put in the ravioli. Simmer
for 3 minutes, then remove with a slotted spoon.

8 Serve the ravioli on a bed of leeks, pour around the sauce,
and garnish with the quail legs, crossed, diced tomato, and
some chives and chervil.

stuffing chicken legs

By boning and stuffing chicken legs you can make something exciting from the parts of the chicken that are often thought of as the least interesting. Although, of course, the legs have a stronger flavor than the breasts, I find chicken a very bland meat that marries well with quite rich combinations of flavors. I like to use a blood sausage stuffing, similar to the one I use to stuff pig's feet. If you don't have any Beef Daube left over to include in the stuffing, you could simply double the quantity of chicken and blood sausage.

I learned how to make blood sausage (*boudin noir* or black pudding) when I was very young and working in a Martinique restaurant. Unfortunately the first time I made the sausages, the chef left me in charge, without properly explaining how to cook them. Instead of poaching them very slowly, I set them boiling and they exploded — about 200 blood sausages all over the kitchen! I don't make them anymore because there are now very strict regulations about their production, but I still love the richness they add to certain dishes. One of my favorite first courses in the brasseries is a simple salad made with dressed leaves, blood sausage, and softly poached eggs.

Sometimes, for a change, we might stuff the chicken legs with a mushroom risotto or pipérade risotto (see page 125).

1 With your fingers, push back the skin and flesh of the drumstick at the thin end.

2 To remove the thighbone, first make an incision along the length of the top of the thigh, cutting right through to the bone.

3 Pull the flesh back, away from the bone, exposing it. Slide a knife underneath the bone to free it further from the flesh.

4 Cut through the joint between the thigh and the drumstick, then snap off the thighbone and discard it.

5 Open out the flesh of the thigh, so that it lies flat on your work surface. Season the chicken leg.

6 Place some stuffing on the area where the thighbone has been removed. Fold over the sides to enclose it.

7 Take a trussing needle and a length of kitchen string, knot one end of the string, and oversew the seam (as though lacing up a boot with a single lace) to seal in the stuffing completely.

You can cook the stuffed chicken legs in any of the following ways:

*To roast, preheat the oven to 425°F. Heat a little olive oil in a large ovenproof sauté pan. Season the chicken legs and brown them all over in the oil. Transfer the pan to the oven and roast about 10–15 minutes, until the juices run clear when the thickest part of the thigh is pierced.

*To confit the stuffed legs, follow the method described on page 74.

*To steam, season and wrap tightly in plastic wrap. Steam for 15 minutes, until the juices run clear when the thickest part of the flesh is pierced.

When the chicken is cooked, by whatever method, remove the string by pulling on the knotted end.

Spit-Roast Chicken Leg Stuffed with Beef Daube and Blood Sausage, with Millefeuille of Apple

serves 4

4 chicken leg quarters

for the stuffing:

½ pound skinless, boneless chicken breast

freshly ground salt and pepper

1 egg

2 cups heavy cream

¹/₂ recipe Beef Daube (page 97)

a little olive oil

6 ounces blood sausage, skinned and chopped

1 garlic clove, chopped

4 shallots, minced

10 basil leaves

small handful of thyme leaves

4 sprigs of thyme

4 bay leaves

for the Caramelized Apple:

2 tablespoons butter

2 Granny Smith apples, peeled and thinly sliced

1 tablespoon confectioners' sugar

1 teaspoon Calvados

½ cup warm chicken demi-glace or 1 cup
   low-salt chicken stock reduced over high
   heat to ½ cup

12 Dried Apple Slices (page 15)

1 Preheat the oven to 425°F.

2 Bone the chicken legs as described opposite.

3 To make the stuffing, first make a chicken mousse: Trim the chicken breast of all fat. Season and chop. Put into a food processor and blend to a paste. Add the egg and blend again for 10 seconds. Scrape the mixture down the sides of the bowl. Add the cream very slowly, scraping down every few seconds, until everything is well incorporated. Pass through a fine sieve.

4 Shred the Beef Daube. Heat a little olive oil in a pan and sauté the daube with the blood sausage, garlic, shallots, basil, and thyme. Season and cool, then mix in the chicken mousse.

5 Stuff the chicken legs with the mixture and roast with the thyme and bay leaves, as opposite.

6 Meanwhile, make the Caramelized Apple: Melt the butter in a pan and add the apple and sugar. Cook over a moderate heat, until the apple is golden and just soft. Add the Calvados and stir over the heat to deglaze the pan.

7 Remove the chicken from the oven and undo the string by pulling on the knotted end. Slice at an angle. Spoon some demi-glace or reduced stock on the plates and arrange the chicken on top. Alongside, make a millefeuille by layering up the Caramelized Apple and Dried Apple Slices. Garnish with the roasted herbs.

For me, the best squabs are the farmed ones that come from Bresse in France. They have a waxy, yellow-gold flesh that takes its color from the corn on which the birds are fed and quite a thick skin, similar to that of a corn-fed chicken. Their flavor is rich, but not gamey.

Normally for roasting you would choose young tender squabs. Those from Bresse are often bred to be quite large, but they still have a good amount of tender meat on them, including the legs, so you can create a more substantial dish with them.

Wood pigeon (and wild doves) on the other hand, have a darker, stronger-flavored flesh. Their breast meat lends itself well to marinating, and can be wonderful. However, wild pigeons have legs like an Olympic sprinter from running around all day, so they can be quite muscular and tough. The legs are best added to game casseroles and slowly cooked in red wine, or chopped up and used to make a rich sauce.

Like most game birds, squab and wild pigeon breasts need to be cooked only briefly or the flesh will dry and tighten up. As with most roasts and all but the smallest of game birds, the squab needs to be left in a warm place to rest for a few minutes after cooking to allow it to recover its juices.

Roast Squab with Red Onion Tarte Tatin

I like to serve roast squab with a tarte Tatin made not with fruit, but with red or sweet white onions, simmered first in milk to draw out any acidity, then cooked in red wine, the deeper the flavor and color the better. We add a dash of grenadine or port a few minutes before the end of cooking time to accentuate the dark color, then glaze the tarts with honey, rather than caramel.

You could make the onion Tatin as an unusual accompaniment for any simply roasted meat; alternatively, when you want to make something more impressive, use it as a base for the carved breasts and legs of a roasted squab, layered up with baby vegetables as we do in the restaurant.

serves 4

4 individual Red Onion Tartes Tatins (page 71)

a little olive oil

4 large squabs or small, tender pigeons

4 sprigs of thyme

4 sprigs of rosemary

4 bay leaves

4 garlic cloves, lightly crushed

for the Red Wine Sauce:

a little olive oil

6 shallots, minced

1 celery stalk, minced

2 garlic cloves, chopped

1 sprig of thyme, chopped

2 fresh bay leaves

6 black peppercorns

4 mushrooms, minced

**1 cup chicken demi-glace or 2 cups low-
   salt chicken stock reduced over high heat to
   1 cup**

**reserved red wine reduction from cooking the
   onions (see page 71)**

freshly ground salt and pepper

1½ teaspoons butter

about 16 baby leeks, to garnish

1 Preheat the oven to 425°F. Prepare the Red Onion Tartes Tatins as described on page 71, up to the point of covering the onions with pastry.

2 Heat the olive oil in a large sauté pan (or two smaller ones). Fry the squabs gently, turning from time to time, until golden brown on all surfaces (make sure the legs, especially, are browned as this meat will take longest to cook).

3 Transfer the squabs to a roasting pan, each balanced on one leg, with a sprig of thyme and rosemary, a bay leaf, and a crushed garlic clove laid over each. Roast for 5 minutes, then turn onto the other legs, and roast for 5 more minutes. Turn onto their breasts and roast for a final 5 minutes, until medium-rare (roast for a little longer if you prefer them more well done). Allow them to rest in a warm place 5–10 minutes after they come out of the oven.

4 After turning the squabs the first time, finish the onion tartes in their pans of honey, and put them in the oven with the squabs when you turn them the second time.

5 Meanwhile, to make the sauce: Heat the olive oil in a pan, add the shallots, celery, garlic, herbs, and peppercorns, and soften without browning. Add the mushrooms and the chicken demi-glace or reduced stock and bubble up until it has reduced by half and coats the back of a spoon. Add the red wine reduction saved from cooking the red onions and bubble up again until reduced to the consistency of heavy cream. Season to taste, then swirl in the butter with a spoon to add shine to the sauce. Strain through a sieve into a clean pan and keep warm.

6 To prepare the garnish: Blanch the baby leeks for about 1 minute in boiling salted water, refresh in cold water, and drain well. Heat a little olive oil in a pan and toss the blanched baby leeks to heat them through. Season.

7 When they are cooked, remove the Tatins from the oven and, with a spatula, carefully flip them over, onion side up, on 4 plates. Be careful not to touch the hot caramel.

8 Serve each squab cut in half lengthwise alongside a tarte Tatin and garnish each plate with a bundle of blanched baby leeks.

red onion tarte tatin

Although we often do use red onions to make this dish — being mild, they suit the treatment — we more generally choose Saint-André onions from France or Vidalia onions, which are white. By the end of cooking, however, they have taken on a rich burgundy color. By all means use red onions, but if you can get hold of Saint-André or Vidalia onions you will find that they are just that bit sweeter.

makes 4

½ pound frozen puff pastry (thawed)

2 red onions or Saint-André, Vidalia, or other sweet white onions (roughly the size of tennis balls)

1¼ cups milk

freshly ground salt and pepper

2 bay leaves

2 cups robust, deeply colored red wine

2 tablespoons red wine vinegar

1 teaspoon chopped fresh thyme

1 teaspoon chopped fresh rosemary

dash of grenadine or port (optional)

4 tablespoons clear honey

1 Preheat the oven to 425°F.

2 Roll the pastry out to a thickness of about ⅛ inch. Cut out 4 circles about 2½ inches in diameter. Pile the pastry circles on a plate and keep in the refrigerator until required.

3 Peel the outside skin from the onions, but leave the base and stem ends intact.

4 Pour the milk into a pan, season with salt and pepper, add the bay leaves and the onions, and bring to a boil. Turn the heat down and simmer for about 10 minutes, until a knife inserted into an onion will go through the outside layers easily, but find the heart still crunchy. Drain.

5 Peel off the next outer layer of onion, and halve each one across the middle.

6 Pour the red wine into a pan, add the red wine vinegar and herbs, and season with salt and pepper. Put in the onions cut side down. Bring to a simmer, then continue simmering for 10 minutes, adding the grenadine or port (if you are using them) after about 5 minutes (don't let the wine boil, as you want to retain its fruitiness). As the wine reduces, roll the onions around from time to time, until they are well coated and almost tender in the center.

7 If you like, strain what is left of the red wine reduction and reserve for a sauce.

8 Put the onion halves on a rack placed over the pan and leave until cold and dry. Trim off the roots and stems.

9 Cover each onion half with a circle of pastry. Slightly tuck the edges underneath the edge of each onion.

10 In a shallow pan, heat the honey until it starts to bubble, then pour a little into each of 4 small tart pans. Place an onion half, in its pastry blanket, on top and bake for about 10 minutes, until the pastry is golden brown and the edges caramelized.

11 Remove the tatins from the oven and, with a spatula, carefully flip them over, onion side up, on 4 plates. Be careful not to touch the hot caramel. Serve with the squab (pages 68–9) or any roast bird.

Roast Squab and Baby Vegetables Layered on Red Onion Tarte Tatin with Red Wine Sauce

This dish might look dramatic, but it is really just another way of serving the tarte Tatin with roasted meat. When you trim the roots and stems from the onions after they have been cooked in wine, take an extra slice away from the stem end. This makes a good flat surface on which to lay the squab.

serves 4

4 individual **Red Onion Tartes Tatins (page 71)**
4 large squab or small, tender pigeons
4 sprigs each of thyme and rosemary
4 bay leaves
4 garlic cloves, lightly crushed
16 baby carrots
16 baby leeks
16 baby turnips
16 pearl onions
Red Wine Sauce (page 69)
4 chervil sprigs, to garnish

1 Make the onion tartes as described on page 71, but take an extra slice off the base when trimming the cooked onions.

2 Cook the squabs with the herbs and garlic as described on page 69.

3 While the tartes and squabs are in the oven, cook the carrots, leeks, turnips, and pearl onions separately in boiling salted water until just tender. Drain and reserve.

4 Start making the Red Wine Sauce as described on page 69 until it is reduced and coats the back of a spoon.

5 Remove the squabs from the oven and carve off the breasts and legs. Keep them warm. Reserve the roasted herbs for garnish.

6 Put the squab bones and trimmings into the pan containing the sauce, then finish the sauce as described on page 69. Keep warm.

7 Remove the tatins from the oven and flip them over onto 4 plates. Press each onion down gently if necessary to make a flat base for a squab.

8 Crisscross the two squab legs on top, then arrange a few baby vegetables on top of them.

9 Next add the two squab breast halves, leaning against each other, plus some more vegetables.

10 Pour a little sauce over the top, and garnish with the reserved roasted herbs, pearl onions, and a sprig of chervil.

confit

You can't beat a well-made *confit* — duck or goose, or even pork, cooked very slowly with herbs in its own fat until the meat is meltingly tender. I also love *rillettes*, which are simply *confit* taken a stage further, so that the meat can be worked into a soft mixture. Since *confit* is such a classic dish, the inventiveness comes from finding new ways of presenting it.

Confit of Duck

serves 4

4 large duck leg quarters, thigh bones removed (either ask
    your butcher to remove the bones or follow the method
    described on page 66)
about 1½ cups coarse sea salt
2 onions, halved
2 carrots, halved
6 garlic cloves, lightly crushed
2 large sprigs of thyme
4 bay leaves
1 pound duck or goose fat, melted

at least 6 hours ahead:

1 Trim all the excess skin and fat from the bottom of the thighs where the bone has been removed, to give the duck legs a shape similar to that of a chicken drumstick. Remove any feather stubble from the skin. You can do this with a burning match, or hold the leg over a gas flame with a fork.

2 Put the duck legs in a shallow dish and cover with sea salt. Leave in the refrigerator for 3 hours to help the meat to tenderize.

3 Preheat the oven to 300°F. Remove the duck legs from the salt and rinse. Place in a roasting pan with the onion, carrot, garlic, thyme, and bay leaves. Cover with the duck or goose fat and leave in the oven for 2 hours, or until the meat almost falls off the bone. Leave to cool and set. Heat through to serve.

4 The confit can be stored in sealed containers in the refrigerator for up to a week until ready to use.

Potted Duck Rillettes with Sour Pickles

In the restaurant we serve *rillettes* with sourdough bread. You can keep the *rillettes* in the refrigerator for several days and you can also make them with rabbit, if you prefer.

serves 4

4 large duck leg quarters, prepared as described
    opposite
10 shallots, peeled and minced
2 garlic cloves, peeled and minced
handful of chives, chopped
10 basil leaves, chopped
sour pickles, to serve
good bread, preferably sourdough, to serve

1 Cook the duck legs as for confit, page 74, leaving them in the oven for about 2$^{1}/_{2}$ hours, until the meat falls completely from the bone.
2 Reserving the fat, remove the skin and bones from the duck.
3 While still warm, use 2 forks or your fingers to break the meat down into a smooth, soft mixture.
4 Put this in a bowl with the shallots, garlic, chives, and basil. Mix together well.
5 Press into 1 large or 4 individual containers, such as ramekins, and spoon some of the confit fat over to create a protective film on the top,
6 Allow to cool and then store in the refrigerator until ready to serve.
7 Serve with the pickles and bread.

Confit Duck Leg, Garlic Crust with Cassoulet Beans

This recipe features *confit* of duck leg baked with a garlic crust and served either with cassoulet beans or, as a variation, with black bean salsa, which we make by simmering soaked black beans in chicken stock for about 1 to 1½ hours with some sweated herbs, garlic, onion, carrot, and celery. When the beans are soft, they are finished with chopped gherkins, extra-virgin olive oil, and some more fresh herbs. Pork belly is mostly cured as bacon. However, some fresh meat is sold trimmed and rolled.

serves 4

for the Cassoulet Beans:

1 heaping cup dried white beans

a little olive oil

4 ounces fresh pork belly, chopped

1 onion, chopped

1 celery stalk, chopped

1 large carrot, chopped

4 garlic cloves, chopped

3 plum tomatoes, chopped

1 bouquet garni

about 2 cups chicken stock, preferably homemade

a few basil leaves, chopped

for the Garlic Crust:

2 slices of dry bread

4 garlic cloves, minced or crushed

small handful of fresh thyme (leaves only)

4 confit duck legs (see page 74)

flat-leaf parsley, to garnish

the night before:

1 Soak the beans in water to cover.

next day:

2 Heat the olive oil in a large heavy-bottomed pan, add the belly pork, vegetables, garlic, tomatoes, and bouquet garni, and sweat gently until the vegetables are soft but not colored.

3 Add the drained beans and cover with the stock. Simmer for about 1½–2 hours, adding a little more hot stock or water if they appear too dry at any time, until they are plumped up and soft. Stir in the basil.

4 Toward the end of the bean cooking time, make the Garlic Crust: Blend all the ingredients in a food processor until finely ground.

5 Preheat the oven to 400°F. Remove the confit duck legs from their fat and roll in the crust mixture.

6 Cook the duck legs in the oven for about 6–8 minutes, until the crust is golden brown.

7 To serve: Pile the beans on plates, top with a duck leg, and garnish with parsley.

cassoulet terrine

For this recipe I looked at the traditional dish of cassoulet, made with *confit* meats, sausage, and white beans, took it apart, then reassembled the elements in a totally different way. I wanted to make a very visual terrine by carefully placing all the ingredients in such a way that when sliced it would look like a slab of marble. I won't pretend, however, that it is quick to make, because all the ingredients have to be prepared meticulously. We even cook the carrot slices that wrap the terrine and the cabbage leaves which are incorporated into it in the duck fat, so that the *confit* character infuses the entire terrine; alternatively, you can simply blanch them, as here. If you find ingredients like lamb tongues and duck gizzards difficult to obtain, you can simply substitute the meat from *confit* duck legs. Toulouse and, to a lesser extent, Morteaux sausages are available from good French delicatessens or gourmet food stores. If you can't find them, use any good-quality fresh sausage, preferably ones flavored with garlic.

serves 10-12

for the Confit:

2 pounds slab bacon or pancetta
10 lamb tongues, blanched (optional)
10 duck gizzards (optional)
4 Morteaux (smoked coarse pork) sausages
4 Toulouse sausages
2 onions, halved
2 carrots, halved
6 garlic cloves, lightly crushed
2 sprigs of thyme
4 bay leaves
1½ pounds duck or goose fat, melted

for the terrine:

4 large carrots, the biggest you can find, plus 6 medium carrots
freshly ground salt and pepper
a little olive oil
4 large Savoy cabbage leaves

3 cups cassoulet beans, cooked as described opposite
2 tablespoons chopped fresh basil
2 tablespoons chopped fresh thyme
2 tablespoons chopped fresh tarragon
2 lamb shanks, cooked as described on page 107, meat stripped from the bone
9 ounces canned, cooked foie gras, cut into cubes (optional)
1 cup lamb or veal stock
4 gelatin leaves or 1 package powdered gelatin, soaked in cold water

for the garnish:

4 ounces pearl onions (about 1 cup)
1 cup finely diced carrots
1 cup cassoulet beans, cooked as described opposite
2 tomatoes
1 cup sherry vinegar
4 ounces goose fat, melted

3 tablespoons truffle oil
1¾ cups vegetable oil
4 garlic cloves, chopped
handful of fresh tarragon, chopped
½ cup chopped chives

early on the day before you want to serve:

1 First confit the meats: Preheat the oven to 300°F. Put the slab bacon, lamb tongues, and duck gizzards if you are using them, and both types of sausage in a baking pan with the onions, carrots, garlic, thyme, and bay leaves. Cover with the duck or goose fat and leave in the oven for 2 hours.

2 Meanwhile, to prepare the vegetables for the terrine: Peel and thinly slice the large carrots lengthwise, preferably using a mandoline slicer. Put the strips of raw carrot in a large bowl, season, and add the olive oil. Reserve.

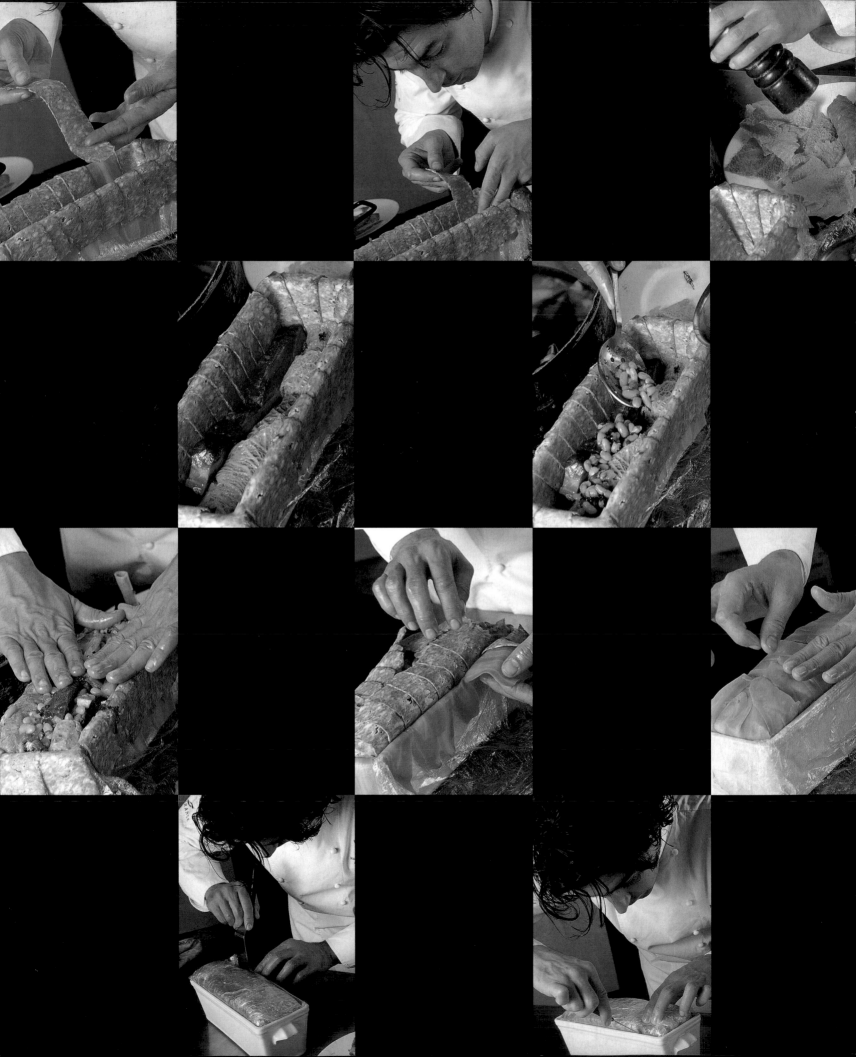

3 Blanch the cabbage leaves in boiling salted water for 1 minute, drain, refresh in cold water, drain well again, and reserve.

4 Cook the medium carrots whole in boiling salted water until just tender and reserve.

5 When the confit meats are cooked, remove them from the oven and leave to cool slightly in the pan. Take out 2 of the Morteaux sausages and reserve. Halve the piece of bacon or pancetta lengthwise.

6 Peel the lamb tongues, if using them, and put them back into the pan of meats.

7 Add the cooked medium carrots, cassoulet beans, and herbs to the pan of meats to warm them through.

8 Slice the 2 reserved Morteaux sausages thinly lengthwise, put them into a separate bowl, season, and add a little olive oil.

9 Season the cabbage leaves.

10 To assemble the terrine: Line a large terrine with 3 layers of plastic wrap, leaving an overhang of about 8 inches on each side to wrap over the top once filled.

11 Line the plastic wrap with the strips of carrot, overlapping them slightly so there are no gaps, and again leaving an overhang all around to pull over the top of the terrine when filled.

12 Repeat using the strips of Morteaux sausage.

13 Place 2 of the Toulouse sausages end to end along the bottom right-hand side of the terrine.

14 Spoon in a line of lamb meat, using half of it along the other side.

15 Sprinkle some cassoulet beans over the top.

16 If using them, place a row of lamb tongues and half the gizzards on top, plus a slice of slab bacon or pancetta.

17 Position the cooked carrots on top and scatter on more beans.

18 Follow with a line of the remaining lamb meat.

19 Wrap the remaining Morteaux sausages in the cabbage leaves and place end to end on top of the lamb. Sprinkle with more beans.

20 Finish with a row of the remaining gizzards, bacon or pancetta, and the 2 remaining Toulouse sausages placed end to end. Top with the foie gras, if using it, and sprinkle the remaining beans over the top.

21 Heat the lamb or veal stock in a pan, add the drained and squeezed-out gelatin leaves or dissolved powder, and whisk well to melt the gelatin thoroughly. Allow to cool slightly, then pour into the terrine.

22 Pull the inner layer of sausage over the top of the terrine, then the final layer of carrot. Pull the overhanging layers of plastic wrap over the top, tucking into the opposite side with a metal spatula. Repeat all the way around.

23 Cut a piece of thick cardboard to fit the top of the terrine. Press down, then wrap the entire terrine as tightly as possible in plastic wrap, place something heavy on top, and leave in the refrigerator for at least 24 hours.

next day, when ready to serve:

24 To make the garnish: Blanch the pearl onions and diced carrots for about 1 minute in boiling water, drain, refresh in cold water, drain again, and put in a bowl with the cassoulet beans.

25 Blanch the tomatoes briefly in boiling water, drop into a bowl of cold water, then remove the skin, quarter, scrape out the seeds, and dice the flesh into $1/4$-inch cubes.

26 Whisk the vinegar, goose fat, truffle oil, and vegetable oil together, and season well.

27 Add one-third of this dressing to the bowl of cassoulet beans, together with the diced tomato, chopped garlic, tarragon, and chives. Season again to taste.

28 To serve: Pour a little of the remaining dressing in the center of each plate. Place a thin slice of terrine on top and brush with a little more dressing. Spoon the dressed beans around the outside.

"You take the idea of a hot rustic cassoulet and transform it into a soft, yielding cold marbled terrine."

rabbit

For many years rabbit was a very unappreciated meat, but recently it has become very fashionable. Unlike much game meat, it has a very delicate flavor, which means it is often used in a similar way to chicken. French rabbits tend to be much bigger than the ones you find elsewhere, and the best are the wild rabbits known as *garenne,* from the French for "warren." Rabbit also makes good *confit* and *rillettes* (see pages 74 and 75).

Confit of Rabbit Leg with Vanilla-Seed Risotto

This is a simple version of a dish devised by my good friend and Novelli Group Executive Chef, Richard Guest, who has been with me since the days at London's Four Seasons. He was looking for a smooth ingredient to take the savory flavor of the rabbit through into a gentle sweetness, but yet avoid masking the delicate taste of the meat with a sharp or overpowering sauce. Vanilla fit the purpose perfectly. To make it even simpler, instead of the *confit* rabbit legs you could pan-fry some slices of rabbit loin, following the method in the restaurant dish that follows.

serves 4

for the Vanilla-Seed Risotto:

a little olive oil

3 shallots, minced

1 garlic clove, minced

1 vanilla bean, split lengthwise into 4

½ cup arborio rice

½ cup sweet white wine, such as Sauternes

1¾ cups chicken or rabbit stock, heated

1 tablespoon butter

1 tablespoon mascarpone cheese

1½ tablespoons grated Parmesan cheese

1 teaspoon chopped chives

freshly ground salt and pepper

4 sprigs of chervil, to garnish

4 confit rabbit legs, prepared and cooked as
   described for duck legs on page 74

¾ cup veal or chicken demi-glace or 1½ cups
   canned low-salt chicken or veal stock
   reduced over high heat to ¾ cup

1 Preheat the oven to 375ºF.

2 To make the risotto: Heat the olive oil in a deep pan and sweat the shallots and garlic with the vanilla bean over low heat, until softened but not colored.

3 Add the rice and stir until well coated. Add the wine and cook, stirring all the time, until the wine has been absorbed by the rice.

4 Gradually add the hot stock, a ladleful at a time. Make sure you stir well after each addition and continue to stir until the liquid is entirely absorbed by the rice before adding more each time.

5 Fold in the butter, mascarpone, and Parmesan. Add the chopped chives and season to taste. Remove the vanilla bean and reserve. Cover the risotto and keep warm.

6 Put the rabbit legs in an ovenproof dish with the veal or chicken stock and cook in the oven for 5–10 minutes, basting regularly, until the meat takes on a rich color and shine. Remove from the oven and keep warm.

7 Place the rabbit legs in the center of the serving plates and spoon the risotto around them. Garnish with chervil and the reserved vanilla beans.

> *"Smooth vanilla takes the savory flavor of the rabbit into a gentle sweetness."*

Rabbit and Vanilla-Seed Risotto with Confit Rabbit Leg, Rabbit Loin, and Vanilla Sauce

This is Richard Guest's dish as it appears on the menu at Maison Novelli. We use red shiso leaves, an Asian herb, to garnish the dish. The leaves have a slightly aniseed flavor, not unlike chervil, but since their main function is decoration, don't worry if you can't find them.

serves 4

Vanilla-Seed Risotto (as previous page)

a little olive oil

freshly ground salt and pepper

4 boneless rabbit loins

4 confit rabbit legs, prepared and cooked as
    described for duck legs on page 74

¾ cup veal or chicken demi-glace or 1½
    cups canned low-salt veal or chicken stock
    reduced over high heat to ¾ cup

for the Vanilla Sauce:

1 cup Muscat dessert wine

1 vanilla bean, split lengthwise

1 garlic clove, lightly crushed

1 teaspoon olive oil

to serve:

a little Basil Oil (page 11)

a few chervil sprigs

red shiso leaves (optional)

1 Preheat the oven to 375°F. First make the risotto as described on the previous page, reserving the vanilla bean strips. Keep warm.

2 Heat a pan and put in a thin film of olive oil. Season the loins and cook them on all sides until golden brown and cooked through, about 6 minutes.

3 Add the strips of vanilla bean reserved from the risotto. Stir around the pan until the seeds from the bean coat the rabbit. Remove the pan from the heat and leave to rest for 3 minutes.

4 Meanwhile, slice the bases from the confit rabbit legs so that they will stand upright, and cook and glaze with the veal or chicken demi-glace or reduced stock as described on the previous page.

5 To make the Vanilla Sauce: Put all the ingredients except the olive oil into a small saucepan and heat gently, so that the liquid reduces slowly to a syrup. Stir in the olive oil and season.

6 Spoon some risotto into the center of each plate and place a confit rabbit leg upright in the center.

7 Carve each rabbit loin into 6–8 slices and arrange these in an overlapping circle on top of the risotto.

8 Dribble the Vanilla Sauce around the edge of the plate and intersperse with drops of Basil Oil and juices from the pan used for glazing the confit rabbit legs.

9 Garnish with the vanilla bean strips used for cooking the rabbit loins, a sprig of chervil, and red shiso if you have it.

venison

I am sure many people have an idea of venison as a very mature wild, pungent meat, which usually has to be marinated heavily and served in winter casseroles. However, modern farmed venison is much younger and very lean, so you can treat tender pieces of loin as you might steak or lamb, serving it medium-rare.

Pan-Fried Venison and Scallops

Like most people who love to eat and to cook, I am always greedy to try every new flavor and concept. Whenever I go out to eat with friends I always want to try what they are having. Often I think that the Asian way of eating is the best, because the custom is to order and try many dishes, instead of having to limit yourself to the conventional first course, main course, and dessert.

Some years ago I started playing around with ideas for combining meat with fish (such as sea bass and chorizo, see page 56), partly so that customers could have more of the flavor of my menu contained on one plate. Of course, there is nothing new in mixing fish and meat — many very old dishes in many cultures combine them in stews, casseroles, and rice dishes — but I wanted to do it using the more modern techniques of pan-frying and broiling.

To make the relationship work you have to be like someone who arranges marriages. You have to understand the character of each partner, and make the match very carefully so that neither one is too dominant nor too aggressive. The perfect relationship is the one in which each ingredient helps to bring out the best in the other.

The delicate sweet scallop is very happy with more robust flavors like venison or lamb. As in this first recipe, you could simply and quickly pan-fry the venison and scallops, then sprinkle on a little herb oil as a finishing touch.

When you have more time you could do as we do in the restaurant and cut the meat into scallop-sized pieces to make brochettes, as opposite.

serves 4

a little olive oil

freshly ground salt and
    pepper

4 boneless pieces of venison
    loin, each about ½ pound

12 sea scallops

Cilantro Oil (page 11)

1 Heat a frying pan until very hot, then add a film of olive oil. When this is also very hot, season the venison pieces and fry them for about 4 minutes on each side for medium-rare. Remove and keep warm.

2 Get the pan good and hot again. Season the scallops and put them into the pan. Pan-fry for 1 minute on each side, until golden brown.

3 To serve, slice the venison thinly and arrange with the scallops. Dribble a little Cilantro Oil over them.

Venison and Scallop Bay Leaf Brochettes

Both the scallop and the venison enjoy spicy flavors, so we serve this brochette with a masala sauce, made with our own combination of spices, finished with fresh cilantro and lime juice. If you have some branches from a bay tree, strip them of their leaves — leaving a few on one end for garnish — and use these as skewers.

serves 4

for the Masala Sauce:

2 tablespoons Masala Spice Mix (page 108)

2 tablespoons butter

6 onions, very thinly sliced

4 garlic cloves, minced

4 tomatoes, chopped

1¾ cups chicken stock, preferably homemade

1 cup heavy cream

1 tablespoon chopped cilantro

juice of 1 lime

freshly ground salt and pepper

4 boneless pieces of venison loin, each about ½ pound

8 medium-sized sea scallops

12 shiitake mushrooms

12 Confit Shallots (page 93)

12 basil leaves

a little olive oil (optional)

Cilantro Oil (page 11), to garnish

1 First make the Masala Sauce: Dry-roast the spice mix briefly in a pan over low heat to release the flavor. Put in a coffee grinder and grind to a fine powder.

2 Heat a little butter in another pan and sweat the onions, garlic, tomatoes, and half the spice mix very slowly until the onions are very soft.

3 Add the stock and reduce slowly down to a thick sauce.

4 Add the rest of the spice mix and the cream, and cook for 15 minutes over a low heat.

5 Pass the sauce through a fine sieve and add the cilantro, lime juice, and seasoning. Keep warm.

6 If using bay leaf branches as skewers, remove all the leaves except for 2 or 3 at one end (keep the leaves for another dish).

7 Slice each venison loin into 3 pieces, roughly the same size as the scallops.

8 Alternate the venison, scallops, shiitake mushrooms, Confit Shallots, and basil leaves on each bay leaf branch or skewer.

9 Either pan-fry in olive oil or broil, either way using a very high heat.

10 Serve with a little sauce and Cilantro Oil dribbled around each plate.

Daube of beef, *pot-au-feu,* braised lamb shanks — these are all dishes which my mother cooked and my grandmother cooked before her, and the food with which every French person has grown up. When they are made with patience and care they are wonderful meals in themselves, but when I see such timeless dishes they seem to challenge me to take hold of them and reinvent them in some new, unexpected and exciting way.

I see a plain *pot-au-feu* and imagine a beautiful terrine made with the tender meat, shot through the center with green lentils and wrapped in brilliant green cabbage leaves. I see a classic beef *daube* and I want to combine it with smooth chicken mousse to stuff a boned chicken leg or pig's foot or a shiny glazed onion...

beef

When you buy the best cuts of beef, you want a good dark color — indicating that the beef has been well aged — with no sinew but a nice marbling of fat throughout the flesh. Sirloin steak should have a good creamy, not too yellow, layer of fat, but rump and tenderloin should have virtually none.

If you can find it, buy Aberdeen Angus beef from Scotland, which most European chefs think is the best there is. When you buy ox-cheek for beef *daube* you may be offered it already lightly salted. Always check and, if this is the case, omit the curing stage of the recipe. However, I firmly believe that it is best to salt your own beef if you can.

Steak Mignonette, Watercress Salad, Béarnaise, and Pommes Frites

This is a dish that people make all over the world, but it is most famous as a French brasserie dish, so when I opened my first brasserie in London I knew it would have to be on the menu. "Steak frites" can often be a disappointment, but when the steak is tender and precisely cooked, the fries are perfectly crisp on the outside and soft inside, and the Béarnaise sauce just piquant, this is a wonderful combination of things to eat.

The same cooking principle you use for pan-frying a scallop or a piece of sea bass applies to steak: first get your pan hot, then put in a thin film of oil and get that very hot too before putting in the steak. When you are cooking a steak rolled in *mignonette* (mixed peppercorns), to get a really good crunchy crust it is important not to disturb the meat until the moment you flip it over onto the second side, and then not again until you take it out of the pan. This is served quite rare.

A good steak is also a well-seasoned one — you need to add salt and pepper before cooking, or, in this case, add salt before coating with the *mignonette*. Some chefs prefer not to salt steak before cooking, as they feel it draws out the juices that you want to seal inside. I believe, however, that if you add your salt once the cooking process has started and the surface of the meat is sealed in the hot fat, the meat will have formed a barrier against the salt and won't absorb it as well.

serves 4

for the Béarnaise Sauce:

2 egg yolks

1 tablespoon white wine

1 teaspoon tarragon vinegar

1 tablespoon chopped tarragon

1 tablespoon water

freshly ground salt and pepper

½ cup (1 stick) butter, cut into cubes

4 filet mignons, each about 6 ounces, at room temperature

1 tablespoon mixed peppercorns

1 tablespoon coriander seeds

salt

a little olive oil

2 large bunches of watercress

a little Sherry Dressing (page 11)

Pommes Frites (page 94)

1 To make the Béarnaise Sauce: Place all the ingredients except the butter in a round-bottomed bowl and set over a pan of simmering water. Whisk in a figure-eight motion as fast as possible until the sauce becomes as thick as whipped cream, then remove from the heat and slowly whisk in the butter piece by piece. If the sauce thickens too much, adjust it by whisking in a spoonful of hot water. Season to taste, and keep warm. Do not allow to boil or the sauce will separate.

2 Pound the steaks out slightly to flatten them. Crush the peppercorns and coriander seeds and put through a fine sieve. Discard the fine powder, as this will be too fiery. Season the steaks with salt and then press the crushed mignonette into both sides of each steak.

3 Heat a heavy pan until very hot, then add the oil and heat until that is very hot. Sear the steaks in it for just 1 minute on each side.

4 Dress the watercress in the Sherry Dressing.

5 Serve the steak with the watercress, Pommes Frites, and Béarnaise Sauce.

Beef Fillet, Wild Mushroom Polenta with Confit Shallots, Cèpe Oil, and Parmesan Crackling

In France, you would probably buy a *tournedos* or *filet mignon* to make a dish like this. These are the very tender round steaks cut from the heart of the tenderloin — you often hear French people call a charming little child a *petit mignon*.

In our restaurant kitchens we wrap whole beef tenderloin very tightly in plastic wrap to form a cylinder, and hang it for a day. Then, when we want to cook it, we slice off individual portions, cutting through the plastic wrap. The plastic wrap is left on until the very last moment to keep the shape of the meat. Before the meat goes into the pan, we remove the plastic wrap, and the meat keeps its perfect shape as it cooks.

serves 4

16 whole shallots

1¾ cups melted duck or goose fat

1¾ cups quick-cooking polenta

a little olive oil

½ pound wild mushrooms, preferably cèpes, chopped

1 shallot, minced

1 garlic clove, minced

4 tablespoons mascarpone cheese

2 ounces foie gras, diced (optional)

2 tablespoons butter

2 tablespoons grated Parmesan cheese

⅔ cup shredded basil leaves

freshly ground salt and pepper

4 filet mignons, each about ½ pound

a little cèpe (porcini) oil

to garnish:

more cèpe (porcini) oil

8 wild mushrooms, quartered

Parmesan Crackling (page 118), molded into a wave shape rather than a basket

a little Cèpe Powder (page 15)

1 Confit the whole shallots by immersing them in duck or goose fat and cooking in the oven preheated to 300°F for 1 hour. Drain and reserve.

2 Turn the oven setting up to 475°F.

3 Cook the polenta according to package directions.

4 Heat a little olive oil in a pan and sauté the chopped mushrooms, shallot, and garlic until lightly colored.

5 Mix the contents of the pan into the hot polenta, along with the mascarpone and foie gras if using it, all but 1 teaspoon of the butter, the Parmesan, and shredded basil. Keep warm.

6 Season the steaks all over.

7 Heat an ovenproof pan until very hot, then add some olive oil, and get that very hot. Put in the steaks and brown on all sides to seal.

8 Add the confit shallots and quartered cèpes, and season again. Add the remaining butter and transfer the pan to the preheated oven to cook for 6–8 minutes.

9 Remove the pan from the oven and leave the steaks to rest for 2–3 minutes. Add a splash of cèpe oil to the pan.

10 To serve: Spoon some polenta on each plate and pile it up quite roughly. Dribble a little cèpe oil over it.

11 Place a steak on top. Garnish each plate with 4 confit shallots and some of the quartered mushrooms.

12 Spoon around a little of the juices from the roasting pan. Top with a wave of Parmesan Crackling and the remaining cèpe quarters, and dust with Cèpe Powder.

pommes frites

As I always say about using all your senses in cooking, I believe that you can actually hear a french fry sing at the point at which it is ready to come out of the fat. It is something I learned in my first job at a bistro in Arras, France. I was the king of the *pommes frites* and the omelets. Not much of a job you might think, but even making french fries can be a quest for perfection.

The two big disappointments with fries are that they are either too soggy or they look good on the outside but aren't cooked in the middle. The way to avoid both of these pitfalls is simply to blanch the fries first to part-cook the potato without crisping it, then raise the temperature and cook again for just long enough to crisp the outside of the potato, without overcooking it all the way through.

Don't cook too many at once, or you will lower the temperature of the oil too much when you add the fries; instead cook in batches.

1 Peel some large waxy potatoes and cut each potato into slices about ½ inch thick, then cut these into strips ¾ inch wide. Try to make sure the fries are of an equal size, otherwise the thinner ones will cook too quickly.

2 Fill your deep-fryer with oil or half-fill a deep heavy saucepan (never fill it further) and heat the oil to 300°F.

3 Lower the fries into the oil (if you are not using a fryer, use a blanching basket) and blanch for about 7–10 minutes, until they are just softened and slightly translucent, but not colored.

4 Remove the fries and drain well on paper towel.

5 Just before you want to serve them, reheat the oil to 350°F, lower the fries into the hot oil again and fry, this time for less than 5 minutes, until they are golden and crisp on the outside, but soft on the inside (test by removing one carefully and breaking it in half). Listen carefully and I swear you will hear them sing!

6 Drain and serve immediately.

beef daube

Beef daube was put on the menu by Jean-Marie Lenfant, one of the original loyal band of chefs that came with me from London's Four Seasons and helped to set up Maison Novelli.

Now Jean-Marie is running Le Moulin de Jean, the mill I bought in Normandy, which is only about 20 kilometers from the farm where his family grows or rears most of their own food, including rabbits. They even make their own Calvados, cider, and Cassis. Jean-Marie's mother loves to feed people and this is the way she and generations of excellent French country cooks like her would half-cure and cook a *daube de boeuf*.

The important thing is to cook the dish for the first part of the process in wine only. It must be a rich mature wine, nothing too young or it will give the dish a sour taste. Only when the meat has taken up the flavor of the wine do you add any stock.

When I began to think about new ideas for the menu at my new restaurant, Les Saveurs, in London's Mayfair, my mind turned to ways of presenting beef daube, beyond using it to stuff chicken legs and pig's feet, dishes that I already had on the menu at my other London restaurants. I came up with the recipe for richly glazed onions stuffed with beef daube that follows.

Traditionally, ox cheeks, the muscles on either side of the steer's jaw, are used for this dish. If you can't find them, use beef chuck, rump, or round instead.

Half-Cured Beef Daube

serves 4

4 ox cheeks or 2 pounds beef chuck, rump, or round

6 cups kosher salt

2 celery stalks, chopped

2 carrots, chopped

2 onions, chopped

1 head of garlic, halved through the middle

2 cups robust red wine

1 cup Madeira

1 cup port

freshly ground salt and black pepper

a little flour

a little olive oil

¼ pound fresh pork belly (see page 76), chopped

pared peel from 1 orange

4 sprigs each of thyme and rosemary

4 bay leaves

4½ cups beef stock, preferably homemade

½ tablespoon butter

2 tablespoons licorice extract (optional)

early on the day before:

1 Trim all the skin and fat from the meat. Cover with the salt and leave for 6 hours, turning regularly.

2 Rinse the meat, put in a large bowl, together with the vegetables and garlic, and pour in the wine, Madeira, and port. Cover the bowl with plastic wrap and leave to marinate in the refrigerator for 24 hours.

next day:

3 Remove the meat and vegetables, reserving the marinade. Pat the meat dry and dust it in a little seasoned flour.

4 Heat some oil in a large heavy ovenproof sauté pan and brown the meat all over. Add the vegetables and sauté for a little longer, until lightly colored.

5 In a separate pan, boil up the marinade to skim.

6 Add the skimmed marinade to the pan with the meat and vegetables, together with the pork, orange peel, and herbs. Cook very slowly on top of the stove for 1 hour.

7 Meanwhile, preheat the oven to 325°F.

8 Add the stock to the pan, cover, and transfer to the oven for 4 hours. The beef is ready once it falls apart when a fork is inserted into it. Remove the meat from its cooking liquid and keep warm.

9 Pass the liquid through a fine sieve into a clean pan and reduce to a sauce-like consistency.

10 To finish the sauce, stir in the butter and any extract.

11 Slice the meat and serve with the sauce and potato or Celery Root Purée (page 98).

Sweet Glazed Onion Stuffed with Beef Daube

We use sweet Saint-André or Vidalia onions for this recipe.

serves 4

4 large sweet white onions (as large as you can find)

2¾ cups red wine

2¾ cups veal demi-glace, or 5½ cups low-salt veal
    stock reduced over high heat to 2¾ cups

½ recipe Beef Daube (see previous page)

a little olive oil

4 ounces foie gras, roughly chopped (optional)

1¼ cups finely chopped shallots

4 garlic cloves, minced

½ cup shredded basil

freshly ground salt and pepper

for the Celery Root Purée:

1 large celery root, roughly chopped

1 large potato, roughly chopped

1 garlic clove, chopped

about 2¾ cups milk

2 tablespoons butter

a drop of truffle oil (optional)

for the Mixed Mushrooms:

a little olive oil

¾ pound assorted wild mushrooms

1 garlic clove, chopped

½ cup shredded basil

1 Preheat the oven to 325°F. Peel the outer layer from the onions.

2 Put the red wine and veal stock in a large pan and bring to a simmer. Add the onions and poach gently until just soft. Remove the onions from the pan, reserving the liquid.

3 Carefully, going in from the top, pull out the onion hearts, leaving a good thick exterior shell to hold the stuffing. Mince the onion hearts.

4 Mince the Beef Daube.

5 Heat the olive oil in a pan, add the minced beef, minced onion, foie gras if using it, shallots, garlic, and basil with some seasoning, and sauté for a few minutes.

6 Carefully stuff each onion with this mixture.

7 Place the onions in a roasting pan, pour the reserved cooking liquid around, and spoon some over each onion.

8 Roast in the oven for about 30–40 minutes, basting regularly, until the onions are glazed and golden brown.

9 While the onions are roasting, make the celery root purée: Put the celery root and potato in a pan with the garlic and enough milk to cover. Season. Simmer until the vegetables are very soft, then drain off three-quarters of the milk.

10 Add the butter and process in a blender until smooth. Season again to taste, add a drop of truffle oil if you like (just a drop, or it will be overpowering), and keep warm.

11 Sauté the Mixed Mushrooms: Heat the olive oil in a pan, add the mushrooms, garlic, and basil, and sauté very briefly until colored.

12 To serve: Place each stuffed onion in the center of a plate and surround with the Celery Root Purée and mushrooms.

Pot-au-feu is one of the oldest dishes in France, and this recipe is quite faithful to the classic version, though I like to add a little truffle oil at the end! Like many such meal-in-a-pot dishes, pot-au-feu traditionally fulfilled several roles: The cooking broth could be served with croutons, the meat and vegetables eaten separately, and any leftover meat could be made into a salad or kept for meatballs or a meatloaf the next day.

It is this last notion that first inspired me to make my spin-off dish of fresh ham hock and lentil terrine. One day, when I was at The Provence Restaurant in Lymington, Hampshire, in the heart of rural England, we had a big party booked. They had asked for pot-au-feu, and then canceled too late for me to stop my meat order, so I was left with a kitchen full of fresh ham hocks. The staff were complaining that they were forever eating casseroles and stews, so I decided to cook the hocks and then make them into a terrine as a change for them. It turned out so well that we decided to develop the terrine further to serve to the customers, adding the lentils, baby onions, and shiitake mushrooms, and wrapping the whole thing in cabbage leaves.

Pot-au-Feu

serves 4

2 fresh ham hocks

2 onions

2 celery stalks

10 black peppercorns

3 bay leaves

1 sprig of thyme, coarsely chopped

1 small head Savoy cabbage, cut into pieces

2 small potatoes (turned, if you like, into barrel shapes)

1 small rutabaga

2 small leeks, trimmed and halved

3 carrots, halved

2 garlic cloves, split in half

6 basil leaves, chopped

freshly ground salt and pepper

to serve:

sea salt

a little truffle oil (optional)

a little garden cress

a little flat-leaf parsley

the day before:

1 Soak the ham hocks in cold water overnight to remove any excess salt.

next day, at least 4 hours before you want to serve:

2 Rinse the hocks well and put them in a pan with 1 of the onions and 1 of the celery stalks, coarsely chopped, the peppercorns, bay leaves, and thyme. Cover with water and simmer for about 3 hours until tender, skimming and replenishing the water as necessary. The classic and best way to test if the meat is cooked is to pull the small bone at the top of the hock, known as the souris or "mouse." If it comes away, then the meat is ready.

3 Remove the hocks from the pan, reserving the liquid. Strain this cooking liquid through a sieve and bring it back

to a boil, then add the remaining onion and celery stalk, halved, along with the rest of the vegetables, the garlic, and basil leaves. Cook until the vegetables are tender.

4 Remove bones and excess fat from the hocks and put the meat in the pan with the vegetables to heat through. Season.

5 To serve: Pile the meat in the center of the plates, arrange the vegetables around the meat, and pour a little of the cooking broth over. Sprinkle with sea salt and, if you like, dribble a little truffle oil over the top. Garnish with garden cress and parsley.

Cabbage-Wrapped Ham Hock Terrine with Sauce Gribiche

serves 10

for the lentils:

½ cup dried green lentils

2 shallots, minced

1 small carrot, minced

1 celery stalk, minced

2 garlic cloves, minced

1 bay leaf

2 cups cooking liquid from the hocks

4 plum tomatoes

6 basil leaves, chopped

a dash of sherry vinegar

1 tablespoon truffle oil

freshly ground salt and pepper

¼ pound baby onions, peeled

6 large Savoy cabbage leaves

a little duck fat

5 fresh ham hocks, cooked as for pot-au-feu
   (page 100)

olive oil

1 pound fresh shiitake mushrooms

1 garlic clove, minced

1 tablespoon clear honey

for the Sauce Gribiche:

1 cup olive oil

½ cup each of tarragon, parsley, and dill

⅓ cup drained capers

1 teaspoon white wine vinegar

whites of 3 hard-boiled eggs, chopped

sprigs of dill, to garnish

well ahead, ideally 2 days before serving:

1 Put the lentils to soak in water overnight. Thorough soaking helps the skins stay on during cooking.

next day:

2 To prepare the lentils: Drain them and put them in a pan with the shallots, carrot, celery, garlic, and bay leaf. Cover with some of the cooking liquid from the hocks, reserving the remainder, and bring to a boil, then turn down the heat, and simmer until the lentils are soft, about 20 minutes. Drain the lentils and leave to cool.

3 While the lentils are cooking, blanch the tomatoes briefly in boiling water, then peel, seed, and chop the flesh. Mix the tomatoes, basil, sherry vinegar, and truffle oil into the lentils, and season to taste. Reserve.

4 Blanch the baby onions for about 1 minute in boiling water, drain. Heat the honey in a pan add the onions and cook slowly, stirring often, until they caramelize. Reserve.

5 Season the cabbage leaves. Heat the duck fat in a pan and fry the cabbage until soft. Remove and reserve.

6 Remove all the bones, fat, and sinew from the ham hocks and reserve the meat.

7 Reduce the reserved cooking liquid from the hocks until it is syrupy. Mix the meat with a little of this syrup and season with pepper.

8 Heat a little olive oil in a pan and briefly sauté the shiitake mushrooms and garlic until softened. Reserve.

9 Place 3 layers of plastic wrap on a work surface, one on top of the other. Cover the plastic wrap with a rectangle of cabbage leaves, about 16 x 10 inches, overlapping to leave no gaps. Cover the cabbage leaves with the pork mixture, leaving a little border at the edges.

10 Mix together the mushrooms, baby onions, and lentils. Spoon the mixture in a strip down the center of the pork mixture.

11 Roll up carefully and tightly like a jelly roll inside the plastic wrap. Twist the ends together tightly, wrap in another layer of plastic wrap, and chill overnight.

on the day of serving:

12 To make the Sauce Gribiche: In a blender or food processor, blend together the oil, herbs, capers, and vinegar. Press the egg through a fine sieve, then stir into sauce and season to taste.

13 Unmold the terrine, unwrap, and slice thickly. Brush both sides of each slice with olive oil.

14 To serve: Place a slice of terrine in the center of each plate and spoon some sauce around it. Garnish with dill and season with freshly ground black pepper.

pig's feet

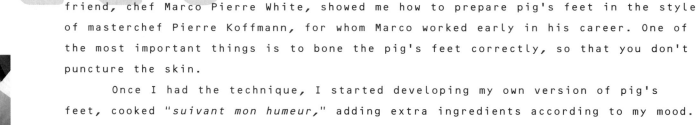

Surprisingly for a Frenchman, I had never cooked a pig's foot in my life until my friend, chef Marco Pierre White, showed me how to prepare pig's feet in the style of masterchef Pierre Koffmann, for whom Marco worked early in his career. One of the most important things is to bone the pig's feet correctly, so that you don't puncture the skin.

Once I had the technique, I started developing my own version of pig's feet, cooked "*suivant mon humeur,*" adding extra ingredients according to my mood. I became crazy about pig's feet, cooking them again and again, until they became better and better and more and more full of flavor. To alleviate the boredom of boning, sometimes fifty feet at a time, we set up a competition in the kitchen to see who could do it the fastest. At first I held the record, then Richard Guest overtook me, with a time of 30 seconds for a single pig's foot!

To the basic chicken mousse stuffing, I add sautéed blood sausage and beef daube. Sometimes I also put in Toulouse sausage that has been poached, skinned, diced, and then fried. I might even add some sautéed wild mushrooms and foie gras or some *confit* ox tongue or Morteaux sausage. On another day I might add some pork from a *pot-au-feu*. The important thing to remember is that whatever you add must be cooked first, because the pig's feet are steamed only for about 12 minutes, long enough to cook the mousse, but not any other raw ingredients.

serves 4

4 fresh hind-leg pig's feet, shank bone removed

1 onion, chopped

2 carrots, chopped

2 celery stalks, chopped

1 leek, chopped

5 garlic cloves, chopped

1 cup each dry white and red wine

a little butter

3½ cups veal stock, homemade or frozen,
    reduced to a syrup

1 recipe stuffing for Spit-Roast Chicken Leg
    (page 67)

4 sprigs of thyme

4 bay leaves

Celery Root Purée (page 98), to serve

1 tablespoon truffle oil

1 First prepare the pig's feet: Singe off the hairs from the skin by holding the pig's foot with a fork over a flame.

2 Place the pig's feet pad-side down on your work surface. Using a sharp knife, make a lengthwise slit down the center. Using the knife to help you, strip and peel away the skin and flesh like a glove, taking care not to rip the skin and working as close to the bone as possible, to expose it completely. Cut through the knuckle joint, then twist and crack off the top of the bone to expose the knuckle bone. Leave this in, as it will be easier to remove later.

3 Put the pig's feet into a large heavy-bottomed pan with the vegetables, garlic, and wines, adding enough water to cover, and simmer gently for 1½ hours, until the pig's feet are soft to the touch.

4 Meanwhile, preheat the oven to 300°F. Put the pig's feet in a roasting pan. Reserve the cooking liquid.

5 Strain the cooking liquid through a fine sieve into a clean pan and reduce by two-thirds. Add the reduced veal stock.

6 Season the pig's feet in the pan and pour the cooking liquid over. Cook in the oven for at least 6 hours, basting regularly, until the pig's feet are

dark brown and shiny, and the cooking liquid has reduced down almost to nothing.

7 Meanwhile, prepare the stuffing as described on page 67.

8 Remove the pig's feet from the oven and, when cool enough to handle, place pad-side down on your work surface. Pull out the knuckle bone.

9 For each pig's foot, take 3 large squares of foil and place one on top of the other. Grease the top square thoroughly with butter. Lay a sprig of thyme and a bay leaf on it. Lay a pig's foot on top, with the intact skin-side down.

10 Open up the pig's foot like a purse and spoon in enough stuffing to fill it out to its original shape. Pull the edges of the skin together to enclose the stuffing and roll up very tightly in the foil, twisting the ends to hold everything in place.

11 Put into a steamer and steam for about 12 minutes, until heated right through.

12 Very carefully unwrap the pig's feet, leaving the herbs in place, and put them on warmed plates, intact skin-side up. Serve with Celery Root Purée, dribble truffle oil and the remaining cooking liquid around, and season.

lamb

Being French, it is natural for me to cook with every part of an animal. It would be very easy to use only prime filets of lamb, but for me it is hard to beat the tender, melting meat that comes from a lamb shank, simmered slowly and then braised in a sauce made of its own stock and enriched with honey, to give it a wonderful shiny glaze.

The shank is the part of the lamb below the shoulder (or sometimes the thigh) and above the foot, containing the leg bone and part of the round shoulder bone. In summer I like to marinate the shanks and then grill them, just as you might cook an overgrown chicken drumstick; they are also delicious braised, then coated in bread crumbs mixed with herbs and spices, and spit-roasted. The braised shanks can be served quite simply with some mashed potatoes and seasonal vegetables, or the Chickpea Salsa opposite. Alternatively, you can dress it up as we do in the restaurant, by adding Pommes Carlos and a Masala Sauce (see page 108).

Classic Braised Lamb Shanks

serves 4

4 small to medium lamb shanks

a little oil

freshly ground salt and black pepper

2 carrots, cut into chunks

2 onions, cut into chunks

2 leeks, cut into chunks

½ pound celery root, cut into chunks

1 head of garlic, broken up

handful of mixed fresh rosemary, bay, and
thyme

for the sauce:

3 tablespoons sliced shallots

2 tablespoons sliced celery

¼ cup sliced button mushrooms

2 tablespoons unsalted butter

1 tablespoon finely chopped fresh mixed herbs,
preferably including tarragon, parsley, and
basil

1 cup red wine

juice of ¹/₂ lemon

2 teaspoons honey

1 Remove excess fat from the lamb and trim the meat away to expose a length of bone. Reserve the meat trimmings.

2 Heat the oil in a roasting pan on the stove. Season the shanks and add to the pan with the vegetables. Brown them quickly all over.

3 While they brown, bring a large pan of salted water to a boil, then plunge the shanks in it for 1–2 minutes. This "blanching" helps the meat to retract around the bone and keep it intact during cooking.

4 Drain and put in a clean pan with the vegetables, garlic, and herbs, along with enough water to cover the meat. Bring to a boil, lower the heat, and simmer gently for about 1½ hours, to the point where the meat is almost falling off the bone. Remove the shanks from the stock and keep warm. Reserve the stock.

5 To make the sauce: Preheat the oven to 325°F. Sweat the sliced vegetables in a little of the butter to soften them without browning them. Add the reserved lamb trimmings and the mixed herbs, and cook for 2–3 minutes more.

6 Pour in the red wine and reduce by half. Add 2 cups of the reserved lamb stock and reduce again by half.

7 Cut the remaining butter into small pieces and whisk these in, a few at a time. Season to taste and strain through a fine sieve.

8 Pour half of this sauce into a roasting pan. Stir in the lemon juice and honey. Add the shanks and coat with this glaze. Cook in the oven for about 20 minutes, removing every 5 minutes to baste.

9 To serve: Remove the shanks from the roasting pan and keep warm. Add the remaining sauce to the pan and heat through. Strain through a fine sieve. Place each shank on a warmed plate and pour on a little sauce. Serve with mashed potatoes and vegetables of choice.

Chickpea Salsa

½ cup dried chickpeas

2 medium tomatoes

a little oil

1 small onion, minced

2 garlic cloves, minced

1 large carrot, minced

1 celery stalk, minced

1 bay leaf

1 sprig of thyme

2¾ cups lamb stock from recipe above or veal
stock

freshly ground salt and pepper

10 basil leaves, shredded

3 tablespoons capers, rinsed and drained

the day before:

1 Soak the chickpeas in water overnight.

next day:

2 Make tomato concassé by blanching, skinning, seeding, and dicing the tomatoes (see page 24). Set aside.

3 Heat a little oil in a pan and sauté the onion, garlic, carrots, and celery gently for a few minutes. Add the bay leaf and thyme.

4 Drain the chickpeas and add to the pan, followed by the tomatoes. Pour in the lamb stock and add water to cover. Cook very gently until the chickpeas are tender and the liquid absorbed, 2–4 hours, replenishing the water as necessary. Season.

5 Just before serving as a bed for the lamb, stir in the basil and capers.

Honey-Glazed Lamb Shanks with Confit Vegetables, Pommes Carlos, and Spicy Masala Sauce

In the brasserie we serve this dish in shallow bowls, with confit vegetables surrounding the lamb shank and the bone decorated with a fried bay leaf and Pommes Carlos — a potato flower made from wafer-thin slices of potato.

serves 4

for the Pommes Carlos:

4 medium potatoes, turned into oval shapes

a little salted butter, melted

for the confit vegetables:

16 shallots

16 shiitake mushrooms

8 baby carrots

4 celery stalks, halved lengthwise

about 2¾ cups melted duck or goose fat

4 lamb shanks, cooked and glazed as on the
   previous page but without the final sauce

for the Masala Spice Mix:

1 tablespoon each ground ginger, cardamom,
   cumin, caraway, coriander, mustard seeds,
   cayenne, and black and white peppercorns

6 whole cloves

2 teaspoons each ground cinnamon, garam
   masala, and salt

2 tablespoons turmeric

sprig of curry leaves

3 pieces of cassia bark

for the Masala Sauce:

2 tablespoons butter

6 onions, very thinly sliced

4 garlic cloves, minced

4 tomatoes, chopped

2¾ cups chicken stock, preferably homemade

1¼ cups heavy cream

2 tablespoons chopped cilantro

juice of 1 lime

8 cherry tomatoes

a little olive oil

4 fresh bay leaves and sprigs of chervil

1 First make the Pommes Carlos: Preheat the oven to 275°. Slice each potato very thinly (preferably with a mandoline slicer). Arrange on a nonstick baking sheet in overlapping circles to resemble flowers (leaving a hole in the center) and brush with melted butter.

2 Cover with a sheet of parchment paper, weight down, and leave in the oven for 1 hour. Remove from the oven for 30 minutes (leaving the oven on), then return to the oven, and leave until slightly transparent, about 10 minutes. Take out of the oven and rest for 2 minutes to crisp up before lifting off with a spatula.

3 Prepare the confit vegetables for the garnish: confit the shallots, mushrooms, carrots, and celery in the goose fat following the instructions for shallots on page 93.

4 Prepare the lamb shanks as on the previous page but, as the bones will become a feature, wrap them in foil before you put the shanks in the oven to keep them white.

5 To make the Masala Sauce: Combine all the ingredients for the Masala Spice Mix in a jar and shake to blend. Dry-roast 2 tablespoons briefly in a pan over a low heat to release their flavors (keep the rest tightly covered for other recipes). Put in a coffee grinder and grind until fine.

6 Heat a little butter in another pan and sweat the onions, garlic, tomatoes, and half of the ground spice mix very slowly until the onions are very soft.

7 Add the stock and reduce slowly by about two-thirds.

8 Add the remaining ground spice mix and the cream and cook for 15 minutes over a low heat.

9 Put through a fine sieve and add the cilantro, lime juice, and seasoning to taste. Add the cherry tomatoes to the sauce to warm them through.

10 Heat a little olive oil in a pan and briefly fry the bay leaves to enhance their color and give a translucent effect.

11 To serve: Place a shank on each plate, pour on the sauce, and surround with confit vegetables and cherry tomatoes. Slide a Pommes Carlos on the end of each shank bone and insert a fried bay leaf into the end of the bone. Secure, if necessary, with a toothpick. Garnish with chervil.

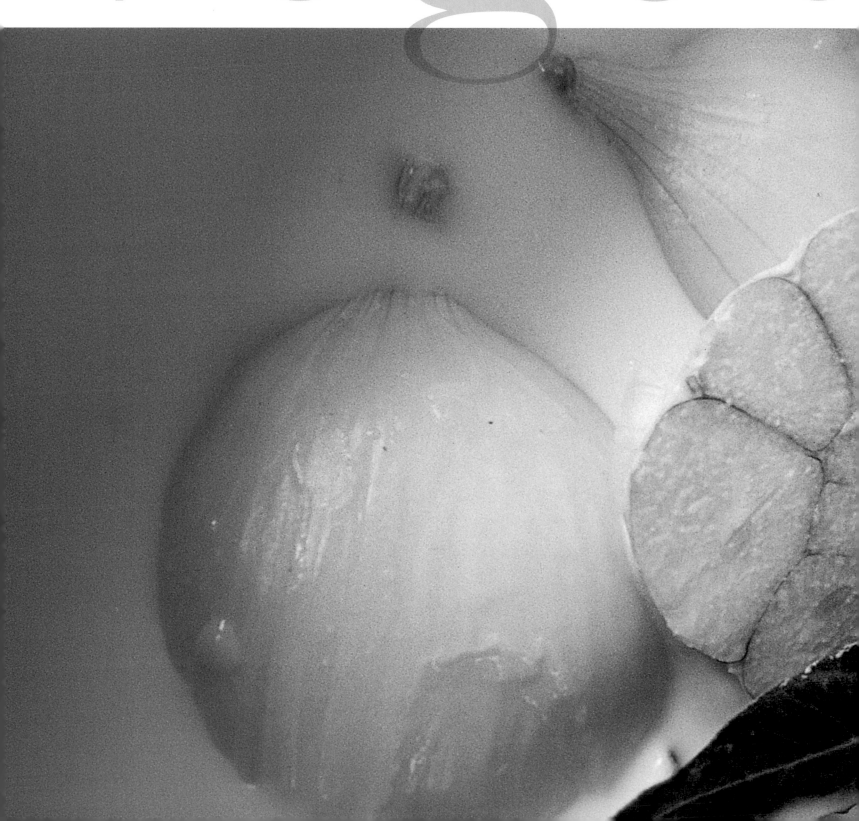

veget

ables

I believe that the chef's job
is to extract as many flavors as possible
from a wide range of ingredients, and that
means working with meat and fish and
vegetables. I love all vegetables, particularly
eggplant, ripe sweet tomatoes, and fennel...
and they are at the core of many of my dishes.
Sometimes I am so pleased with the flavors that
I add no meat or fish — for example,
the Goat Cheese Terrine with Eggplant and Red
Pepper Caviar — but I do not set out to create
vegetarian dishes. I have not been trained to
cook that way. I think that to
cook well, you have to cook what you like
to eat yourself. What lifts you above
the pressures of the kitchen is the joy
of creating something that excites your
own tastebuds. So if I make a gazpacho
soup I cannot help visualizing it with
a *tian* of crab; a pea soup with a
little foie gras; a crêpe filled
with wild mushrooms bound in
chicken mousse...

I still think my mother makes the best soups in the world. She simply puts the vegetables in a pressure cooker with some water and cooks them for 10 minutes only. This preserves all the flavor and nutrients. Cook soup for a long time and you simply end up with stock.

The first of these soups is a gazpacho that can be served very simply, or dressed up with a *tian* of crab.

Gazpacho Soup

Gazpacho soup is one of the simplest things in the world to make, but the secret of a good one is to find the correct balance between sweet and sour, using the right proportion of sugar to vinegar. You may have to adjust the sugar level slightly according to the sweetness of your tomatoes — these quantities are based on the sweetest, reddest, most over-ripe ones it is possible to find.

serves 4

1 pound very ripe cherry tomatoes
2 large over-ripe tomatoes
2 teaspoons white wine vinegar
2 tablespoons truffle oil
½ cup olive oil
2 teaspoons sugar
freshly ground salt and pepper
chopped cilantro, to garnish

1 Process all the ingredients except the cilantro in a blender, thin with water if necessary, and season to taste. Put through a fine sieve and chill for at least 2 hours.
2 Pour into bowls and garnish with the chopped cilantro.

Gazpacho Soup with White Crab and Cilantro

serves 4

4 large red ripe tomatoes

4 ounces fresh crab meat, carefully
    picked over

2 tablespoons Anchovy Mayonnaise (page 35)

2 tablespoons diced cucumber

2 tablespoons chopped chives

2 tablespoons chopped cilantro

4 mint leaves, chopped

dash of truffle oil

dash of lime juice

freshly ground salt and pepper

Gazpacho Soup (opposite)

for the garnish:

4 tablespoons Red Pepper Reduction (page 12)

4 sprigs of cilantro

a little red shiso or garden cress

1 Blanch the tomatoes briefly in boiling
water, transfer to a bowl of cold water, drain,
then carefully remove the skins.

2 With a sharp knife, cut a slice from the base
of each tomato (not the stem end). Using a
1-inch pastry cutter, cut out a neat round
from each of these slices. Cut down the side of
each tomato and open it out into a long strip.
Scrape out the seeds.

3 Using your cutter again, cut out 2 more
rounds from each strip of tomato, then cut the
remaining tomato flesh into small dice
(concassé). Reserve all the tomato rounds.

4 To make the tians: Combine the crab meat
with the diced tomato, mayonnaise, cucumber,
herbs, truffle oil, and lime juice. Season to taste.

5 Take the cutter and place it in the center of
a soup bowl. Place one of the tomato rounds
cut from a tomato strip inside. Pack some crab
mixture on top, pressing down firmly, then
press another tomato round cut from a

tomato strip on top of that. Follow with
another layer of crab, pressed well down, then
carefully lift off the cutter. Top each little
tower of crab with a round cut from a tomato
base.

6 Carefully pour the Gazpacho Soup around
the crab tians, dribble some Red Pepper
Reduction in a design over the surface of the
soup, and serve garnished with cilantro and
red shiso or garden cress.

Pea Soup with Pancetta

This is another very simple soup that can be made more elaborate when you feel like it by adding foie gras and a cappuccino topping. By crisping up the pancetta before adding it to the soup, you add a lovely smokiness.

serves 4

a little butter

1 small onion, chopped

2 ounces pancetta, chopped

3 cups shelled fresh or frozen peas

1 garlic clove, coarsely chopped

3½ cups light chicken stock, preferably
    homemade

1 sprig of mint

freshly ground salt and pepper

pinch of sugar

1 Heat a little butter in a large pan, add the onion, and sweat gently until translucent.

2 Get a frying pan very hot, then add the pancetta, and quickly fry until crisp.

3 Add the pancetta to the other pan, along with the peas and garlic, and cook for a few minutes.

4 Pour in the stock and bring to a simmer. Cook until the peas are very tender. Add the mint, season, and add the sugar.

5 Blend until smooth, then put through a fine sieve and serve hot.

Pea and Cured Foie Gras Cappuccino Soup

serves 4

3 ounces canned, cooked foie gras

freshly ground salt and black pepper

Pea Soup with Pancetta (above)

4 tablespoons milk, crème fraîche, or cream, warmed through
    in a pan

2 tablespoons unsalted butter

Cèpe Powder (page 15)

1 Lay the foie gras on a sheet of plastic wrap and season, then roll up very tightly, and chill until firm.

2 Reheat the soup and adjust the seasoning if necessary. Warm 4 soup bowls.

3 When ready to serve the soup, slice the wrapped foie gras into rounds about ½ inch thick. Remove the plastic wrap.

4 Place a round of foie gras in the bottom of each of the bowls. Pour the soup on top.

5 If you have a cappuccino frother, froth up 4 tablespoons of warm milk with the butter; if not, whisk some warm cream or crème fraîche with the butter using a hand-held blender. Spoon on top of the soup.

6 Dust the tops with Cèpe Powder to make the soup resemble a large cappuccino.

Along with tomatoes, eggplants are among my favorite vegetables. Though some people say you don't need to salt them before cooking, I prefer to, to draw out any bitterness. Just halve them lengthwise or cut them into chunks if you are making Eggplant Caviar (see below), put them on a plate, and sprinkle well with coarse sea salt. Leave them for half an hour, then wipe with paper towel before cooking.

It is important to season eggplants well before you cook them, as they soak up seasoning in much the same way as they take in olive oil. Once the eggplants are cooked and oily, it is very difficult to get the seasoning to penetrate.

Eggplant Caviar

This is a classic way of cooking eggplant. The technique takes its name from the eggplant seeds, which look a little like fish roe when the flesh is cooked. Most chefs purée the cooked eggplant, which enhances the caviar effect, but I prefer to serve it in chunks. That way it makes a great base for dishes such as Andalouse of Sole (see page 50). You can also cook red bell pepper along with the eggplant, as in the Goat Cheese Terrine on page 120.

It is best to choose slender eggplants, as these have fewer seeds and less of a bitter aftertaste than the fatter, germinating eggplants. They also cook quicker. I have given a cooking time of somewhere between 30 and 60 minutes, which will vary according to the size of the eggplants you buy.

You can make Eggplant Caviar and store it in a sealed jar in the refrigerator for up to two weeks, provided it is completely covered in the olive oil in which it has been cooked (replenish this with extra olive oil, if necessary).

serves 2 as a side dish

1 slender eggplant
freshly ground salt and black pepper
5 bay leaves
a few basil sprigs
1 sprig of rosemary
1 sprig of thyme
1 whole head of garlic, halved
3 shallots, chopped
pinch of sugar
a little olive oil

1 Preheat the oven to 375°F.

2 Cut the eggplant into chunks and salt them as described above.

3 Wipe the eggplant pieces to remove excess salt and place them in the center of a large piece of foil, along with the herbs, garlic, and shallots. Season well, sprinkle with sugar, and dribble with the oil, then fold up the foil to make a loose package, crimping the edges to seal.

4 Bake in the preheated oven for 30 minutes to 1 hour, until the eggplant flesh is like jelly. Use as an accompaniment to meat or fish, or as required in other recipes.

Spicy Eggplant Salad with Parmesan Crackling

This is an example of my way of building up a dish using favorite ideas and garnishes. You will find all the techniques used here in other recipes or in the first chapter of this book.

serves 4

about 1 cup grated Parmesan cheese

Sun-Dried Tomato Juice (page 12)

mixed salad leaves

Sherry Dressing (page 11)

4 tomatoes

Eggplant Caviar (page 116), cut into chunks
 rather than slices, and dusted with a little
 Masala Spice Mix (page 108) before cooking

mixed herbs, such as basil, chives, and tarragon

cilantro leaves, to garnish

1 Make Parmesan baskets by sprinkling one-fourth of the cheese evenly over the bottom of a 6-inch omelet pan. Heat until the cheese has turned light golden and almost stopped bubbling. Ease out of the pan and, while still warm, press gently into a teacup. When cool and crisp, carefully remove from the cup. (Note: The shinier underside of the Parmesan crackling – i.e. the side in contact with the pan – should form the outside of the basket) The crackling may also be formed into other shapes. Make 3 more baskets in the same way.

2 Put the Sun-Dried Tomato Juice in a pan and reduce to a syrup. Reserve.

3 Dress the salad leaves in the Sherry Dressing. Mound in the center of each plate.

4 Blanch the tomatoes briefly in boiling water, drop into a bowl of cold water, then remove the skin, quarter, scrape out the seeds, and dice the flesh into ¼-inch cubes.

5 Mix the chopped Eggplant Caviar with the chopped tomato, sun-dried tomato syrup, and herbs. Spoon into the Parmesan baskets.

6 Nestle a basket on top of each mound of leaves, and garnish with cilantro.

> *"Season eggplants well before you cook them."*

Tarte Fine of Eggplant, Tapenade, Chorizo, and Mozzarella

serves 4

1 eggplant

freshly ground salt and pepper

1 sheet of frozen puff pastry, thawed

a little olive oil

4 tablespoons prepared tapenade

½ pound mozzarella cheese, sliced thinly

½ Spanish chorizo sausage, sliced thinly at an
   angle

for the Tapenade Dressing:

1 tablespoon black olive paste

5 tablespoons olive oil

6 basil leaves, chopped

1 garlic clove, chopped

a drop of truffle oil

mixed salad leaves and herbs

Sherry Dressing (page 11)

Red Pepper Reduction (page 12)

1   Salt the eggplant as described on page 116.
Preheat the oven to 425°F.

2   Cut the puff pastry into 4 rounds, about 5
inches in diameter, and prick all over with a
fork to prevent them from rising.

3   Bake in the preheated oven for about
5 minutes until golden. Reserve.

4   Wipe the eggplant and slice into rounds

about ⅛ inch thick. Season with pepper.

5   Heat some olive oil in a pan and pan-fry the
eggplant slices until lightly colored and soft.

6   Spread the tapenade over the puff pastry
rounds. Lay the slices of mozzarella on top.
Overlap the rounds of eggplant and chorizo on
top of the mozzarella.

7   Bake in the oven until the chorizo begins to
crisp and the mozzarella begins to melt.

8   To make the Tapenade Dressing, mix all the
ingredients together.

9   To serve: Place a tart in the center of each
plate. Dress the leaves and herbs in the Sherry
Dressing and pile this salad on top. Dribble the
Red Pepper Reduction and dressing around.

Goat Cheese Terrine with Eggplant and Red Pepper Caviar

Although this is technically not a terrine, because it is rolled up to form a cylinder rather than packed into a dish, it follows the same technique of pressing together layers of differently flavored and textured ingredients. This is one of my favorite dishes — wafer-thin slices of potato and celery root wrapped around goat cheese, basil, bell peppers, and eggplant.

I like to use a full-flavored yet not overpowering goat cheese, such as Sainte-Maure or Boucheron, together with a layer of mozzarella, not for its flavor, which is too subtle to get itself noticed, but for the smoothness and gloss it adds to the terrine.

serves 10

Eggplant Caviar (page 116), made using
2 large eggplants and 3 large red bell peppers, not cut into chunks but prepared as described in Step 1
4 large waxy potatoes
1 celery root
freshly ground salt and pepper
a little olive oil
1 pound goat cheese
a little butter
2 big bunches of basil (about 6 ounces)
10 ounces mozzarella cheese, thinly sliced
flour, for dusting

for the garnish:
mixed salad leaves and herbs, to serve
a little Sherry Dressing (page 11)
10 Dried Tomato Slices (page 15)
halved cherry tomatoes
halved black olives
Tapenade Dressing (page 119)

1 Preheat the oven to 400°F. Cut each eggplant in half lengthwise, then from each half cut out the flesh containing the seeds and open out to leave 2 strips of skin with about ¼ inch of flesh attached. You should end up with 4 strips in all.

2 Cook the eggplant strips, with the whole peppers, as for Eggplant Caviar (page 116).

3 When the caviar is ready, cut the peppers down one side, open them out, peel, and scoop out the seeds, to leave 3 large strips of pepper. Pat the pepper and eggplant slices with paper towel to remove excess oil.

4 Peel the potatoes and celery root and slice them very thinly, preferably with a mandoline slicer, keeping the vegetables separate.

5 Season the potato and celery root rounds, sprinkle with olive oil, and bake separately on oiled nonstick baking sheets for about 10 minutes, until just beginning to color and soften. Drain and allow to cool.

6 Cut the rind from the goat cheese, lay it between 2 sheets of plastic wrap, and flatten with a rolling pin.

7 Stack 3 sheets of foil on top of each other. Smear the top layer of foil with a little butter and season. Arrange a rectangle of overlapping potato rounds about 16 x 12 inches on the foil, then season. Cover half of the potato with the celery root rounds. Cover the celery root with strips of pepper down one side and eggplant down the other. Season. Next cover the pepper and eggplant with overlapping leaves of basil. Follow with a layer of goat cheese, seasoning each layer. Finish with a layer of mozzarella slices. Roll up carefully in the foil to resemble a jelly roll.

8 Wrap the roll as tightly as you can in several layers of plastic wrap, twisting the ends to hold everything in place. With a sharp knife, puncture the plastic wrap through to the foil all over, then take hold of the twists of plastic

wrap at each end and squeeze, to force the excess vegetable juices out of the holes. Keep on doing this until no more juice comes out (ideally hang it up in a cool place for 24 hours). This is important, as the terrine will later be sliced and pan-fried, and if there is too much liquid inside, the outer wrapping of potato won't crisp up nicely. Leave the wrapped terrine in the refrigerator until ready to use.

9 Slice the terrine thickly (about 1½ inches) through the plastic wrap, then return the slices to the refrigerator for 10 minutes.

10 Remove the plastic wrap and dust the slices with flour. Heat a large pan until hot, then add a little olive oil. When that is hot, pan-fry the slices of terrine on both sides.

11 Dress the salad leaves and herbs with the Sherry Dressing.

12 Place a slice of terrine on each plate. Garnish with the leaves and herbs and a slice of dried tomato. Arrange the halved cherry tomatoes and olives around the plate and dribble some Tapenade Dressing around.

pipérade

On vacation in the Pays Basque in the French Pyrénées many years ago I first ate *pipérade*: vegetables, like bell peppers and zucchini, with olives, Bayonne ham, and scrambled eggs. Sometimes it is a chunkier dish, made with halved, very softly boiled eggs, the yolks of which melt into the vegetables.

Of course, I couldn't just simply adopt such a dish for my menu. My brain began churning over ways to take the essence of the dish and present it in a new way. Instead of eggs, I substituted rice for one dish, pasta for another. To take my family tree of dishes even further, I began experimenting with *pipérade* risotto as a stuffing for chicken or rabbit legs, both of which regularly appear on my menus.

Classic Pipérade

Pipérade in its traditional form is a great dish for a brunch or light lunch. This is how I would make it...

serves 4

for the Pipérade Vegetables:

½ cup olive oil

1 large zucchini, sliced at an angle

1 medium eggplant, sliced at an angle and then each slice halved

12 small shallots, peeled

8 baby fennel (or slender fennel bulbs, quartered lengthwise), trimmed

2 red bell peppers, seeded and cut into large strips

2 yellow bell peppers, seeded and cut into large strips

1 head of garlic, cloves separated and peeled

½ cup Sun-Dried Tomato Juice (page 12)

freshly ground salt and black pepper

good handful of black olives

20 basil leaves

4 warm soft-boiled eggs, peeled and halved

handful of mixed fresh herbs, to serve

1 Prepare the Pipérade Vegetables: Heat the olive oil in a pan, add the vegetables, garlic, and Sun-Dried Tomato Juice, and season. Cover with a tight-fitting lid and cook over low heat until the vegetables are just softened.

2 Remove the vegetables from the heat and add the olives and basil to warm through.

3 Carefully arrange the vegetables on 4 plates with the soft-boiled eggs and serve garnished with fresh herbs.

Penne with Pipérade and Mozzarella

serves 4

1 pound penne

a little olive oil

2 large tomatoes

½ cup Sun-Dried Tomato Juice (page 12)

2 tablespoons butter

2 tablespoons prepared tapenade

20 small cherry tomatoes

4 ounces mozzarella, cubed

Pipérade Vegetables (as above)

salt and pepper

10 basil leaves, chopped

for the garnish:

fresh herbs, such as basil and chervil

shavings of fresh Parmesan cheese (made using a vegetable peeler)

1 Cook the penne in boiling salted water with a spoonful of olive oil until just *al dente*. Drain and reserve.

2 Briefly blanch the large tomatoes in boiling water, refresh in cold water, then remove the skins. Quarter them, scrape out the seeds, and dice the flesh into ¼-inch cubes.

3 Put the Sun-Dried Tomato Juice in a pan and reduce to a syrup.

4 Melt the butter in a sauté pan, add the tomato syrup and tapenade, and heat through. Add the pasta and stir until the butter coats it.

5 Add the cherry tomatoes, mozzarella, and Pipérade Vegetables. Stir until the vegetables have warmed through and the cheese has melted and coated the pasta. Season and stir in the diced tomatoes and basil.

6 Serve garnished with herbs and Parmesan shavings.

Pipérade Risotto with Red Pepper Reduction

serves 4

a little olive oil

5 shallots, minced

1½ cups arborio rice

5 tablespoons dry white wine

2¾ cups hot vegetable stock

1¼ cups **Sun-Dried Tomato Juice (page 12)**

½ tablespoon prepared tapenade

1 cup mascarpone cheese

⅔ cup grated Parmesan cheese

1½ cups shredded basil

Pipérade Vegetables (page 122)

for the garnish:

a little **Red Pepper Reduction (page 12)**

dash of truffle oil

4 Dried Eggplant Slices (page 15)

4 Dried Tomato Slices (page 15)

strips of **Parmesan Crackling (page 118)**

fresh mixed herbs, such as basil sprigs and red shiso

1 Heat the oil in a pan, add the shallots, and sweat gently until translucent.

2 Add the rice and stir to coat.

3 Add the white wine and cook, stirring all the time, until the wine is absorbed.

4 Gradually add the hot vegetable stock, a ladleful at a time. Make sure you stir well after each addition and continue to stir, until the liquid is entirely absorbed by the rice, before adding more.

5 Add the Sun-Dried Tomato Juice and continue to cook until this is also absorbed and the rice is soft.

6 Stir in the tapenade, mascarpone, Parmesan, and basil.

7 To serve: Arrange the risotto on plates, top with Pipérade Vegetables, then dribble the Red Pepper Reduction and truffle oil around, and garnish with dried eggplant and tomato, the cracklings, and the herbs.

Some people say that you shouldn't wash mushrooms — the point is that you shouldn't let them soak up water. Mushrooms are about 75 percent water, and if you wash them and leave them damp they soak up the excess like a sponge. Then, just like scallops, they will let this moisture out when you pan-fry them.

If you clean the mushrooms well with a small brush, then, just before you cook them, put them under running water, drain them, and dry them well, they should be fine.

When you pan-fry different types of wild mushroom, start with the biggest and toughest, then gradually add the smaller, finer ones, finishing if you like with the Japanese enoki, lovely tiny white caps with long stems, which take only around 10 seconds to cook.

Wild Mushrooms in Crêpes

In the north of France, where I was brought up, we have a local dish of mushrooms in mornay sauce wrapped in a crêpe. When I began cooking at The Provence Restaurant in Lymington, close to England's New Forest, with its natural treasure of wild mushrooms, I began to elaborate on this.

I would go out at dawn during the mushroom season, armed with baskets and tripping over roots and brambles in the half-light, searching for cèpes, chanterelles, etc., then I would bring them back to the kitchen and experiment with new ideas.

The first recipe given here is for a simple dish of wild mushrooms wrapped in crêpes. The second, which appears on my restaurant menus, is a result of those early-morning cooking sessions: a richer, more elegant variation on the same theme, made with chicken mousse and served with both a mushroom and a port sauce.

serves 4

for the crêpes:

1 cup all-purpose flour mixed with a
   pinch each of salt and pepper

1¼ cups milk

1 whole egg, plus 1 extra yolk, beaten

1 tablespoon sunflower or other
   flavorless oil

handful of poppy seeds

olive oil

for the Mushroom Mixture:

2 pounds mixed cremini and wild
   mushrooms, stems removed

a little olive oil

1 tablespoon chopped shallots

1 garlic clove, minced

⅔ cup chopped fresh basil

½ cup chopped fresh tarragon

¼ cup chopped chives

1 To make the crêpes: Sift the seasoned flour into a bowl. Make a well in the center and add the milk, beaten egg, and oil. Gradually incorporate the flour to make a smooth batter. Stir in the poppy seeds.

2 Heat a crêpe pan, then pour in a thin film of oil. When that is hot, pour a thin circle of crêpe batter into the center of the pan and swirl so that the batter spreads over the entire surface. Cook briefly until the underside is golden when you lift up the edge. Flip over and cook until the second side is golden. Slide onto a plate and keep warm. Cook 3 more in the same way.

(Leftover batter can be refrigerated for 2–3 days.)

3 To prepare the Mushroom Mixture: Clean and slice the mushrooms.

4 Heat the olive oil in a pan and sweat the shallots and garlic gently until softened. Then turn up the heat and add the mushrooms with half the herbs. Sauté briefly and season. Drain. Put the drained mushrooms in a bowl with the remaining herbs and mix well.

5 Pile some mushrooms on each crêpe and roll up or fold as you wish.

Steamed Wild Mushroom Gâteau with Crêpes, Port Sauce, Porcini Oil, and Parmesan Crackling

serves 4

4 crêpes (pages 126–7)
Mushroom Mixture (pages 126–7)

for the Chicken Mousse:
½ pound skinless, boneless chicken breast
freshly ground salt and pepper
1 egg
2 cups heavy cream

for the Mushroom Sauce:
a little olive oil
½ cup minced shallots
2 garlic cloves, minced
½ cup minced celery
2 ounces mixed herbs, such as thyme and
    rosemary
4½ cups chicken stock, preferably homemade
1¼ cups heavy cream
4 ounces canned, cooked foie gras, diced
    (optional)
1 tablespoon butter, cut into cubes

for the Port Sauce:
a little oil
½ cup minced shallots
2 garlic cloves, minced
½ cup minced celery
1 sprig of thyme
1 bay leaf
1 cup port

½ cup Madeira
½ cup veal stock, preferably homemade
1 tablespoon butter, cut into cubes, plus more
    for greasing the ramekins

for the garnish:
a little olive oil
handful of wild mushrooms
cèpe (porcini) oil
Parmesan Crackling (page 118)
sprigs of chervil

1 Make the crêpes and prepare the Mushroom
Mixture, reserving the mushroom stems and
drained juice for the sauce.

2 To make the Chicken Mousse: Trim the
chicken of all fat. Chop coarsley and season.
Put into a food processor and blend to a paste.
Add the egg and blend again for 10 seconds.
Scrape down the sides of the processor bowl
with a spatula. Add the cream very slowly,
turning the machine off every few seconds to
mix again with the spatula, until everything is
well incorporated. Pass through a fine sieve.

3 Add the Chicken Mousse to the Mushroom
Mixture and combine.

4 Place each crêpe in a buttered and seasoned
3-inch ramekin, so that the crêpe overhangs
the edges. Fill with the Mushroom Mixture,
then fold the overlapping edges of the crêpe
over the top to enclose the filling completely.
Wrap each ramekin with plastic wrap, put

them in a steamer, cover and steam for 30
minutes.

5 Meanwhile, to make the Mushroom Sauce:
Heat the olive oil in a pan and sauté the
shallots, garlic, celery, minced mushroom stems,
and herbs, until the shallots are softened.

6 Add the chicken stock and reserved
mushroom juice, and reduce by three-quarters.

7 Add the cream and reduce again by half.

8 Pass through a fine sieve into a clean pan.
Stir in the foie gras, if you are using it, and the
butter. Keep warm.

9 To make the Port Sauce: Heat a little olive
oil in a pan and sauté the shallots, garlic,
celery, and herbs.

10 Add the port and Madeira and reduce by
three-quarters.

11 Add the stock and reduce again until the
sauce coats the back of a spoon.

12 Pass through a fine sieve into a clean pan,
and stir in the butter.

13 To prepare the garnish: Heat a little oil in a
pan and quickly sauté the mushrooms.

14 Place a steamed mushroom gâteau in the
center of each plate, and scatter the Mushroom
Mixture around and on top. Pour a little of
each sauce around the plate. Dribble on a little
cèpe oil and garnish with Parmesan Crackling
and chervil.

carrots

Carrots are such humble things and yet, if you buy them carefully, you can extract so much flavor from them and with a little imagination you can construct something very delicate and impressive. Look for small, brightly colored carrots that are not at all woody.

Steamed Lettuce and Carrot Gâteau with Hollandaise

This is a simpler version of the restaurant dish that follows. In this one you just make a purée of carrots, herbs, garlic, Emmental cheese, and cream, and steam it in molds lined with blanched lettuce. In the second recipe you enhance the purée with some carrots that have been caramelized in honey and olive oil, and garnish the dish with baby carrots coated with Orange and Cardamom Reduction.

serves 4

2 heads romaine lettuce

freshly ground salt and black pepper

1 pound carrots, chopped

⅔ cup shredded fresh basil

½ cup chopped fresh tarragon

3 garlic cloves, chopped

3 tablespoons heavy cream

¾ cup grated Emmental cheese

3 eggs

butter for greasing the molds

Hollandaise Sauce (page 46)

1 Select enough large lettuce leaves to line four 5-ounce dariole or timbale molds or custard cups. Dip the leaves for a second in boiling salted water, drain, refresh in cold water, drain again, and reserve.

2 Cook the carrots in boiling salted water until just tender and drain.

3 Put them in a blender with the herbs and garlic and 1 tablespoon of the heavy cream and process until you have a smooth purée.

4 Add the grated Emmental and season well.

5 Mix the eggs and the remaining cream together, then add to the carrot mixture.

6 Grease the molds or custard cups with a little butter, then line with the blanched lettuce leaves.

7 Spoon in the carrot mixture, then cover with plastic wrap.

8 Place in a steamer, cover and steam for about 30 minutes, or until the mixture has set.

9 Meanwhile, make the Hollandaise Sauce as described on page 46.

10 Remove the molds or cups from the steamer, carefully take off the plastic wrap, and unmold a carrot gâteau on each plate.

11 Serve with the Hollandaise Sauce.

Steamed Lettuce and Caramelized Carrot Gâteau

serves 4

2 heads romaine lettuce

1 pound carrots

freshly ground salt and black pepper

1 tablespoon olive oil

1 tablespoon clear honey

⅔ cup shredded fresh basil

½ cup chopped fresh tarragon

3 garlic cloves, chopped

5 tablespoons heavy cream

1 cup grated Emmental cheese

3 eggs

a little butter

Hollandaise Sauce (page 46)

for the garnish:

12 baby carrots, boiled until tender

2 tablespoons Orange and Cardamom Reduction (page 11, reserving the cardamom pods for garnish)

Basil Oil (page 11)

sprigs of chervil

chives

1 Reserve any small lettuce leaves for garnish, then blanch enough large ones to line four 5-ounce dariole or timbale molds or custard cups as opposite.

2 Cut half of the carrots into cubes of about ½ inch. Sprinkle with salt, put into a steamer, and steam for about 8 minutes, or until just *al dente*.

3 Meanwhile, chop the remaining carrots and cook in boiling salted water until just tender.

4 Put the olive oil and honey in a pan over low heat, add the cubed carrots, herbs, and garlic, and toss well to coat. Cook until the carrots are soft and sticky. Remove the pan from the heat.

5 Drain the boiled carrots, then purée with 1 tablespoon of the heavy cream. Add this mixture to the honeyed carrots and, while still warm, mix in the grated Emmental. Season well.

6 Mix the eggs and the remaining cream together, then add to the carrot mixture.

7 Grease the molds or custard cups with a little butter, then line with the blanched large lettuce leaves.

8 Spoon in the carrot mixture, then cover with plastic wrap.

9 Place in a steamer and steam for about 30 minutes, or until the mixture has set.

10 Meanwhile, make the Hollandaise Sauce as described on page 46.

11 To make the garnish: Heat the Orange and Cardamom Reduction in a pan, add the baby carrots, and toss well until they are coated.

12 Remove the molds or cups from the steamer, carefully take off the plastic wrap, and unmold a carrot gâteau on each plate.

13 Remove the baby carrots from the Orange and Cardamom Reduction, reserving this, and arrange 3 on top of each gâteau. Serve with a little Hollandaise Sauce, dribble some Basil Oil and the remaining reduction around, and garnish with the reserved cardamom pods, any small lettuce leaves, chervil, and chives.

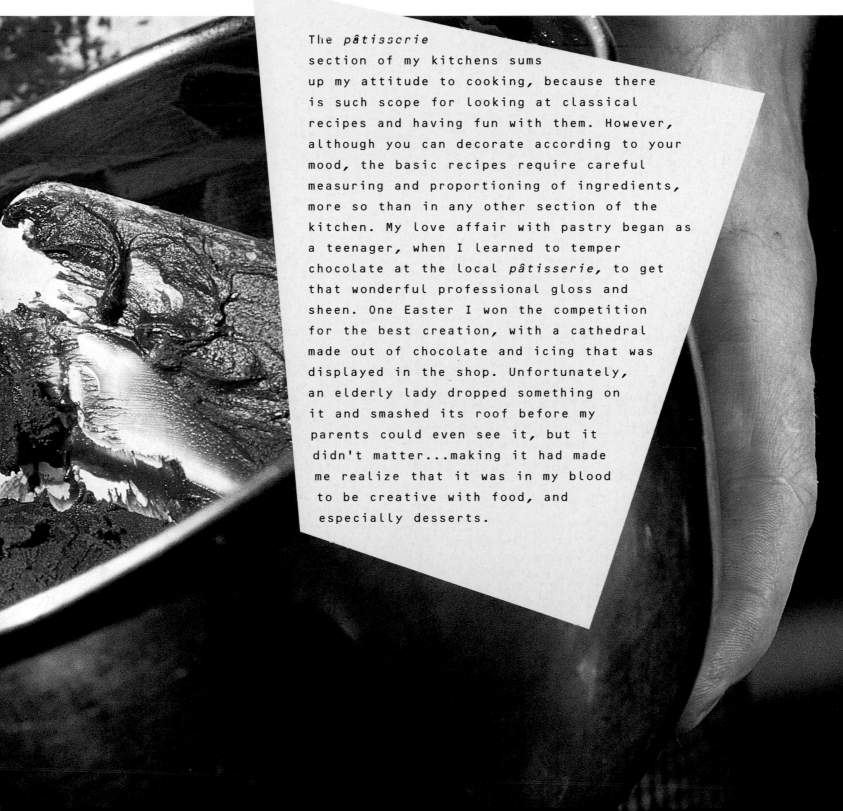

The *pâtisserie*
section of my kitchens sums
up my attitude to cooking, because there
is such scope for looking at classical
recipes and having fun with them. However,
although you can decorate according to your
mood, the basic recipes require careful
measuring and proportioning of ingredients,
more so than in any other section of the
kitchen. My love affair with pastry began as
a teenager, when I learned to temper
chocolate at the local *pâtisserie*, to get
that wonderful professional gloss and
sheen. One Easter I won the competition
for the best creation, with a cathedral
made out of chocolate and icing that was
displayed in the shop. Unfortunately,
an elderly lady dropped something on
it and smashed its roof before my
parents could even see it, but it
didn't matter...making it had made
me realize that it was in my blood
to be creative with food, and
especially desserts.

Some of the best ideas in cooking happen by accident. The idea of a tart cooked upside down, with the fruit underneath the pastry, then turned the right way up, was made famous by the Tatin sisters, who ran a restaurant in Lamotte-Beuvron, near Orléans in France, at the turn of the century. One story is that they were in a hurry and, instead of making a classic apple tart with *crème pâtissière*, they simply put the sugared apple into the tart pan and covered it with pastry. When it was baked, they then flipped it over, and discovered the wonderful caramelized surface of the apples, which has given the dish its endless appeal.

My grandmother used to make enormous tartes Tatins in great big pans with handles. When she turned them over the fruit would fly out everywhere. Take it from me, it is much easier to handle small individual ones, as we do in the restaurant!

The classic tarte Tatin is made with halved apples covered with pastry. We sometimes make one with a whole Pink Golden Delicious apple, peeled and cored. These days, though, most chefs make a more elegant tart with apples cut into quarters, arranged in a circular pattern. Granny Smith apples are best as they hold their texture and flavor.

A perfect tarte Tatin has a combination of crisp pastry, firm but properly cooked fruit, and crunchy caramel. Traditionally, the fruit is caramelized by putting butter and sugar into the Tatin pan, then adding the apples, covering them with puff pastry, and starting the cooking process on the stove. When the butter and sugar begin to bubble and turn golden, the pan is transferred to the oven.

I make the caramel separately, then pour it into Tatin pans lined with parchment paper, before arranging the fruit. This gives a dark, crunchy, mirror-like caramel glaze to the fruit, while the parchment paper stops the caramel from sticking to the pan, and makes it easier to unmold the tart.

We have a whole repertoire of Tatins, made with different fruits, even

banana and strawberry, which you might think are impossible to make without the fruit turning to purée! When we created the recipes, we first put the fruit in the oven without the pastry to see how long we could cook them without them disintegrating. Then we experimented with the pastry rolled out to different thicknesses, until we found the cooking times to match.

Apple Tarte Tatin

makes 4 individual tarts

2 tablespoons unsalted butter, cut into cubes, plus more for
   greasing
4 sheets of frozen puff pastry, thawed
6 Granny Smith apples
½ cup granulated sugar
confectioners' sugar, for dusting

to serve:
Vanilla or Caramel Ice Cream (pages 150 and 152)
Caramel Springs (page 17)

1 Line the bottom of 4 individual 4-inch round Tatin pans or 4-inch baking tins with rounds of parchment paper. Grease the paper with a little butter.

2 Roll the puff pastry out into circles about 4 inches in diameter and ⅛ inch thick.

3 Peel the apples, core them, and cut them into quarters.

4 Heat the granulated sugar with 2 tablespoons of water in a heavy-bottomed saucepan and cook very gently until the resulting caramel is light gold.

5 Remove from the heat and add the cubed butter, stirring well until it is completely incorporated.

6 Pour a thin layer of caramel on the bottom of each lined pan or mold. Pack the apple quarters in a circular pattern on top of the caramel.

7 Drape a circle of pastry over the top, then tuck it in well to encase the apple completely. Leave to rest in a cool place for 20 minutes, so that the pastry won't shrink when it goes in the oven.

8 Preheat the oven to 450°F. Dust each circle of pastry with a little confectioners' sugar, and bake for 18–20 minutes, or until the pastry is golden brown and the apples soft.

9 Remove the tarts from the oven and leave to rest for 1 minute to let the caramel cool and set slightly.

10 Remember that hot caramel burns the skin badly, so be careful when you turn out your tarts. To do so, place a dessert plate over the top of each pan and, with a twist of the wrist, very carefully flip pan and plate over together, so that the tart ends up, apple-side upward, on the plate. Remove the paper.

11 Serve, if you like, with a scoop of ice cream on top and some Caramel Springs. Dust the whole plate with confectioners' sugar.

Banana Tatin

Banana Tatin is the brainchild of Filip Tibos and Mike Ouchbakou, who were my talented pastry chefs at London's Four Seasons. When we were frantically busy in the kitchen, I used to keep going by eating bananas, which I stole from them. One day they presented me with a banana tarte Tatin. It was a very daring thing to try, because banana turns to pulp so quickly when it is cooked. I had never liked cooked banana up to that point, but I loved this immediately. The important thing is to use very firm bananas.

Follow the recipe for Apple Tarte Tatin on the previous pages, but roll the pastry out into thinner circles (about 1/16 inch) and, instead of apples, slice 6 bananas into cylinders about 1 inch in length. Pack these upright on top of the caramel with one in the center and the rest around, like petals. Bake at 425°F for 15 minutes.

Serve, if you like, with Rum and Raisin Ice Cream (page 150), and decorate with Banana Crisp (below).

Banana Crisp

To make enough to decorate 4 desserts: Preheat the oven to 250°F. In a food processor, process 1 banana to a smooth purée, then mix in the juice of 1/4 lemon and 1/2 tablespoon of confectioners' sugar. Spread the mixture thinly over a nonstick baking sheet and put in the oven for about 3 hours, until the mixture is completely dried out. Remove the

sheet from the oven and, while the banana mixture is still warm, ease it out gently with a spatula. Leave flat on a clean work surface until cool and crisp, then break into pieces and use as you like.

Strawberry Tatin

Make as for Banana Tatin, but use large, very firm strawberries and bake for 20 minutes. Serve, if you like, with Vanilla Ice Cream (page 150).

Fig Tatin

Around May, we are able to get deep purple French figs, which are firm, yet ripe and fruity, just right for tarte Tatin. At other times of the year we use green figs, which must be cooked longer to bring out their sweetness. Make the Fig Tatin as the Strawberry Tatin above, substituting 3 whole figs for the strawberries. If using purple French figs, bake for about 15–20 minutes; for green figs, bake for about 25 minutes. Serve, if you like, with Caramel Ice Cream (page 152).

Pineapple Tatin

Make as for Apple Tarte Tatin (previous pages), substituting a ring of fresh pineapple, cut to about 5/8 inch thick, for the apples, and poach the rings first in stock syrup (page 157) for about 15 minutes. Serve, if you like, with Coconut Ice Cream (page 150).

crème brûlée

The secret of a good crème brûlée is in the making of the custard, which must be absolutely smooth. When you boil the cream and milk you need patience to let it come to a boil very slowly. Then, when you add the cream and milk to your egg yolks and sugar, again you must do it very slowly and gently, whisking all the time, otherwise you will end up with something that resembles scrambled eggs.

When the brûlées are ready to come out of the oven (I don't think you need to set the molds in a protective pan of hot water at this temperature, but if you are not sure of your oven then by all means use one), they should be set, but still wobble like a gelatin dessert. Once they hit the cool air, they will become more solid. If you leave them in the oven any longer, they will become too stodgy when cool.

Some people like a thick brûlée crust on a crème brûlée, but I think it should be a thin surface that will crack sharply when you break it with a spoon. We glaze vanilla or mandarin brûlée with superfine sugar, which forms a glassy, brittle surface. For the richer-flavored brûlées, such as coconut or almond, we use raw brown sugar, which has a slightly softer and more crunchy texture.

Vanilla Crème Brûlée

serves 4

1 cup heavy cream
½ vanilla bean, split
⅔ cup milk
7 egg yolks
**½ cup superfine sugar, plus a little extra
   for glazing**

1 Preheat the oven to 250°F.
2 In a pan, bring the cream, vanilla bean, and milk to a boil. Remove the pan from the heat and allow to cool slightly.
3 In a bowl, mix together the egg yolks and sugar.
4 Add the hot cream-and-milk mixture to the bowl slowly, mixing well. Pour through a fine sieve into 4 deep 2½-inch ramekin dishes.
5 Bake for 50–60 minutes, until the surface is just firm, but the brûlées are still a little liquid (check each one at regular intervals, and remove as necessary).
6 Leave to cool, then chill for 2–3 hours.
7 Sprinkle a layer of sugar all over the top, then tip the ramekins and tap the sides gently to let the excess sugar fall off, leaving a thin film of sugar on the top.
8 Either put under a preheated broiler or use a blow-torch to caramelize the sugar. As the sugar melts, tilt the ramekins slightly to spread it all over the surface. You should end up with a thin, golden layer that will crisp up as it cools down.

Coconut Crème Brûlée

Make as for Vanilla Crème Brûlée, but use 1¼ cups heavy cream, 5 tablespoons coconut milk, 1 tablespoon Malibu (rum and coconut liqueur), 6 egg yolks, and ¼ cup sugar. Sprinkle on raw brown sugar, rather than superfine sugar, for the glaze.

"Smooth custard beneath a glassy, brittle surface."

Mandarin Brûlée

Making a citrus fruit brûlée requires a little care, as the acidity of the fruit doesn't naturally mix with milk. We first reduce the mandarin juice with sugar to a thick syrup, before combining it with the milk and cream.

serves 4

2 cups mandarin juice (about 15 mandarin
    oranges), plus grated peel of 3 mandarin
    oranges
heaping ½ cup sugar, plus a little for glazing
1 cup heavy cream
⅔ cup milk
¼ vanilla bean, split
7 egg yolks

for decoration (optional)
4 Tuile Cigars (page 143)
8 Caramel Springs (page 17)

the day before:

1 Put the mandarin juice and peel in a pan with 2 tablespoons of the sugar and bring to a boil, then turn the heat down and simmer until reduced to around 1 teaspoon of thick syrup.

2 Put the cream, milk, and mandarin syrup in a pan with the vanilla bean, scraping in the seeds, and bring to a boil. Remove the pan from the heat and allow to cool.

3 In a bowl, mix together the egg yolks and remaining sugar. Add the cream and milk mixture slowly, mixing well. Leave to cool, then chill overnight, so that the flavors infuse.

next day:

4 Preheat the oven to 230°F. Pass the brûlée mixture through a fine sieve into 4 ramekin dishes and proceed as for Vanilla Crème Brûlée (opposite).

5 If decorating with Tuile Cigars, insert them into each caramelized top as soon as you remove it from under the broiler or have finished using the blow-torch, while the caramel is still soft. As it sets hard, it will keep the cigar in place. Decorate with Caramel Springs.

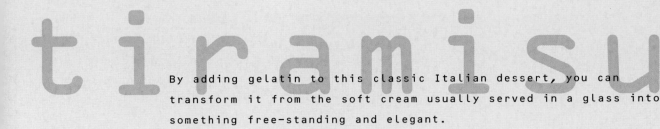

tiramisu

By adding gelatin to this classic Italian dessert, you can transform it from the soft cream usually served in a glass into something free-standing and elegant.

serves 6

3 egg yolks

½ cup sugar

9 ounces (1 cup plus 2 tablespoons) mascarpone cheese

1 cup heavy cream

2 gelatin leaves or ½ package powdered gelatin, soaked in a little cold water for 5 minutes

1 small cup of espresso or strong coffee

2 tablespoons Kahlúa

six 2½-inch-diameter rounds of light sponge cake about ¼ inch thick (you can buy ready-made sponge and cut it to shape or make your own génoise sponge)

for decoration:

a little cocoa powder

White Chocolate Sauce (optional, page 152)

Dark Chocolate Sauce (optional, page 152)

1 In a bowl, whisk the egg yolks with the sugar until pale. Add the mascarpone and mix well.

2 Whip the heavy cream until it just begins to thicken, then add this to the mixture.

3 Transfer 2 tablespoons of the mixture to a pan and heat gently. If using them, squeeze excess liquid out of the soaked gelatin. Add these to the pan or the powdered gelatin solution, and stir until melted. Add to the rest of the cream, mixing well.

4 Mix the coffee and Kahlúa in a bowl. Dip the sponge rounds briefly in this mixture, then put them at the bottom of 4 deep 2½-inch metal rings.

5 Pour in enough mascarpone mixture to come to the top of each ring and chill for about 2½ hours until set.

6 Dust the top of each tiramisu with cocoa powder, carefully slide the rings off, and serve, if you like, with a mixture of White and Dark Chocolate Sauces.

Tiramisu Boat with Three Sauces

In a flight of fantasy for the restaurants, we partner the simple tiramisu with tuile, caramel, and dessert sauces, to make an extravagant model boat!

serves 6

6 individual Tiramisu (see above)

Tuile mixture (page 143)

cocoa powder, for coloring

Caramel (page 17)

6 Caramel Springs (page 17)

Crème Anglaise (page 153)

Coffee Sauce (page 153)

Dark Chocolate Sauce (page 152)

1 Make the Tiramisu as above and keep in the refrigerator until ready to serve (do not dust with cocoa powder until the last minute).

2 Make up the tuile mixture, including some with cocoa powder for icing.

3 Preheat the oven to 350°F. To make the boat, make some stencils as follows: Take one sheet of cardboard and cut out 4 long petal shapes. These will form the base of each boat. Spread some tuile mixture over the top and carefully remove the cardboard. With your chocolate mixture, pipe a line all the way around each petal shape, a little in from the edge of the tuile.

4 Bake for about 4 minutes until the tuile is just beginning to color.

5 Remove from the oven and, while still warm, bend the ends of each

boat upward slightly. Leave to cool.

6 Take another sheet of cardboard and cut out 5 squares, each approximately 2½ inches. This is enough for the sails for one boat. Spread the mixture over the cardboard stencils, then remove it carefully and pipe an edging around the sails with chocolate tuile. Then, with a skewer, make a hole toward the center-top and bottom of each sail (the rigging will be threaded through here, see picture). Bake as above.

7 When the sails come out of the oven and while still warm, drape them over the length of a rolling pin to curve them. Leave to cool.

8 Repeat until you have 5 sails for each boat. If you have enough baking sheets you can make them all at once, rather than in batches, but it may then be difficult to mold all the sails while they are still warm; in that case, just put them back in the oven briefly until they are pliable again.

9 To make the caramel masts, trail some caramel up and down over some wax paper. You need enough to make 3 masts per boat. Leave the caramel to harden, then snap into equal lengths.

10 Remove the Tiramisu from the refrigerator and dust the top of each with cocoa powder. Place a "boat" in the center of each of 6 plates, then place a Tiramisu in the center of each boat.

11 Insert 3 caramel masts into each Tiramisu, one vertical, the others pointing forward and backward at angles. Thread 2 sails onto the back and center masts, using the holes in the tuile. Thread one sail on the front. Slide a Caramel Spring over the end of each mast.

12 Make a sea around each boat by pouring on a little of each sauce, then run the handle of a spoon through them to create a wave pattern.

tuiles

There is nothing new about *tuile*. It is a classic cookie mix that has been used over the years to accompany all kinds of desserts. What is exciting is how you work with it as, while it is warm, it can be fashioned into whatever shape you like. If you prefer, you can use a food processor to make the mixture.

Tuile Cookies

makes about 24

0 tablespoons unsalted butter
¾ cup confectioners' sugar
½ tablespoon vanilla extract
whites of 3 eggs
1 cup all-purpose flour

1 Preheat the oven to 400°F.

2 In a bowl, cream the butter, sugar, and vanilla together. Gradually beat in the egg white, then fold in the flour until you have a smooth paste. Chill for about 2 hours.

3 Place small spoonfuls of the mixture about 4 inches apart on a nonstick baking sheet, then spread these out into rounds with a spatula.

4 Bake for about 4 minutes until the mixture is just beginning to color (keep checking).

5 Remove from the oven and leave to cool very slightly until you can handle them. Shape the rounds by draping them over the length of a rolling pin or as described below. Leave until completely cool and set, then lift off gently. You can keep the tuiles in an airtight container for up to a week.

Other Shapes:

Baskets

Depending on the size you want, drape your warm rounds of baked tuile over the top of a clean bottle or gently press them inside a tea or custard cup and leave until cool.

Stencils

Take a piece of clean cardboard and cut out the shapes you want: say, flowers or leaves. Lay the cardboard stencil on your baking sheet and spread the mixture over the top. Lift off the cardboard carefully before baking.

Cigars

Take a piece of clean cardboard and cut out a series of oblongs about ½ inch wide and 8 inches long. Proceed as for the stencils above. When the tuile comes out of the oven and is cool enough to handle, wind each strip loosely around a sharpening steel or wooden spoon handle. Leave until cold, then slide off.

Chocolate Edging

The tuile shapes can be decorated by mixing a little of the tuile mixture with a little cocoa powder. This can be piped around the edges of flower shapes, or along the center of the strips for "cigars," before the tuile goes into the oven.

chocolate

When I was a child, before I went to bed at night I used to eat a piece of pure dark chocolate to help calm me down. Then, as now, I found it difficult to sleep, because my mind would always be racing, full of ideas and plans. My mother found that the best chocolate, made with 70 percent cocoa solids and no added sugar, can have a relaxing effect.

Chocolate Marquise

This is a classic dessert that can be served simply on its own, or with a little white chocolate sauce, cream, or crème anglaise and a dusting of confectioners' sugar and/or unsweetened cocoa powder. However, we use it as a base for one of the dishes that seems to have earned me the most publicity, the Jack-in-the-Box.

serves 6

six 2½-inch-diameter rounds of light sponge cake about
  ¼ inch thick (you can buy ready-made sponge and cut it
  to shape or make your own génoise sponge)
a little brandy
4 ounces good-quality bittersweet dark chocolate
whites of 5 eggs
¼ cup superfine sugar
1¼ cups heavy cream, lightly whipped to soft peaks

for decoration:
halved strawberries
tiny mint sprigs
confectioners' sugar
unsweetened cocoa powder

1 Brush the rounds of sponge lightly with a little brandy and place one in the bottom of each of six 2½-inch round molds.
2 Break the chocolate into squares and put these in a bowl. Place this bowl over a pan of hot water set over a very low heat and let the chocolate melt, stirring constantly. Do not let the chocolate boil or its flavor and texture will be impaired.
3 In another bowl, whisk the egg whites until they form soft peaks. Fold the sugar into the egg whites, then fold in the whipped cream. Fold this mixture into the chocolate.
4 Spoon the resulting chocolate mousse into the molds and refrigerate to set, about 2 hours.
5 When ready to serve, run a warmed knife around the outside of each of the molds and then invert them to turn out the marquises onto 6 serving plates. Decorate with strawberry halves and mint sprigs, then dust lightly with confectioners' sugar and cocoa powder.

Jack-in-the-Box

The first time I made the Jack-in-the-Box was the best. Sometimes, like scoring a perfect goal in soccer, everything comes together at the right time and you achieve something quite special that can never be reproduced in quite the same way. The idea obviously came from the child's toy, which I wanted to recreate with food; but, unlike wood and fabric, of course, food is perishable. Changes in temperature, movement, heat, and the weight of the decorations destroy it minute by minute from the moment it is made.

That first Jack-in-the-Box was made spontaneously, but then came the nightmare of trying to teach the other chefs in my kitchen to copy it quickly and in large quantities, without someone having to go out and tell the customers, "Sorry you will have to wait twenty minutes, because the chef is going crazy trying to get the caramel right!"

When you are not in a pressurized kitchen, though, it is a fun dessert to make. One day, when you have the time and you are feeling creative, why not try it? The caramel "sides" to the box can be made in advance and stored in an airtight container.

serves 4

4 Chocolate Marquise, as opposite

neutral oil, such as corn, for greasing
2½ cups sugar
2 tablespoons light corn syrup
4 tablespoons ground almonds

for decoration:

3 tablespoons confectioners' sugar
⅔ cup roasted hazelnuts
16 Caramel Springs (page 17)

1 Make the Chocolate Marquise as described opposite, but in 2½-inch square molds, and chill.

2 Preheat the oven to 350°F.

3 To make the sides of the box: Lay out a sheet of parchment paper on a work surface and oil it lightly.

4 Put the sugar and corn syrup in a heavy-based pan and heat gently until a golden caramel forms. Remove from the heat and carefully pour the caramel over the oiled parchment paper.

5 Leave to cool until brittle, then smash two-thirds into little pieces with a rolling pin. Put the caramel pieces in a blender with the ground almonds and process to a powder with the consistency of granulated sugar.

6 Have ready a large nonstick baking sheet. Sprinkle the powdered caramel very thinly over the baking sheet to an even layer covering an area of 15 x 12½ inches. Put the sheet in the preheated oven for about 3 minutes. Keep checking it and remove the moment the caramel has melted again and resembles a sheet of glass.

7 Leave to cool just 1 minute, then, using a clean ruler and a sharp knife, score it across in a grid of lines 2½ inches apart horizontally and vertically, forming 30 squares. You will actually need only 24 of these squares, but the extras allow for the possibility of any splintering or otherwise getting damaged. Score 10 of the squares in half again into 2 equal rectangles. When the caramel is completely cold, snap along the scored lines to break the caramel into squares, plus the 20 rectangles (again, you will need only 16 rectangles; the others are extras).

8 Put the reserved caramel into a pan and melt it gently. You will use this as glue and glaze for assembling the box and for coating the hazelnuts. Remove the Chocolate Marquise from the refrigerator. Turn each out of its mold as described opposite and place each in the center of a large plate.

9 As you work with the caramel, constantly dust your fingers with confectioners' sugar, to keep the caramel from sticking to them. Stick a square of caramel to each side of each marquise (these should cling to the chocolate), then "weld" the corners together, using a hot knife.

10 Take 4 of the rectangles, dip one long edge of each into the warmed caramel, and stick one to the top of each "side" of the box, to resemble an open lid. Repeat with the remaining boxes.

11 Dip the hazelnuts into the caramel and pile them into the top of each box.

12 Very carefully position the springs to look as though they are jumping out of the top of the box. Dust the whole thing with confectioners' sugar – and pour yourself a large brandy!

Chocolate Dessert

Most chefs have a version of a chocolate dessert that is firm on the outside, but when cut open reveals a soft, silky chocolate center. There are many tricks to help achieve this effect, but this is one of the simplest. All that is required is to bake the dessert to a precise timing that allows the outside to become firm, leaving the center soft.

When we cook this dessert it is the only time we have an alarm clock in the kitchen. When the desserts are ready they will rise up in the middle and feel firm to the touch. Don't leave them in the oven any longer, as once they begin to crack, it means the center will start to firm up too, ruining the whole point of the dessert.

serves 6

5 eggs, plus 5 extra yolks

½ cup sugar

9 ounces good-quality bittersweet dark
    chocolate, broken up

1 cup (2 sticks) unsalted butter, plus a little
    extra for greasing molds

scant ½ cup all-purpose flour, sifted

the day before:

1 In a bowl, beat together the eggs, egg yolks, and sugar until pale.

2 Meanwhile, melt the chocolate and butter gently in a bowl set over a pan of hot water. Remove from the heat. Slowly add to the egg mixture, beating until smooth. Fold in the flour.

3 Pour into buttered 5-ounce molds before it begins to firm up. Chill overnight.

next day:

4 Preheat the oven to 350°F. Bake for 10–15 minutes, until the centers dome and feel dry (check regularly). Unmold and serve.

Hot and Cold and White Chocolate Plate

serves 6

Tuile mixture (see page 143)

White Chocolate Sauce (page 152)

Dark Chocolate Sauce (page 152)

6 Chocolate Desserts (as above)

White Chocolate Ice Cream
    (page 150)

6 Caramel Springs (page 17)

6 sprigs of red currants

confectioners' sugar

6 sprigs of mint

flat block of bittersweet chocolate

1 Make 6 Tuile Cookies in the shapes of spoons with tapering handles, using stencils, as shown on page 143. While still warm, bend the spoon "handles" (see picture opposite).

2 Dribble the chocolate sauces in zigzags across the serving plates. Place a Chocolate Dessert off center and a tuile spoon alongside. Place a scoop of White Chocolate Ice Cream on the tuile spoon. Decorate with the Caramel Springs.

3 Decorate with some red currants dusted with confectioners' sugar, a sprig of mint, and some chocolate curls made by shaving strips off a block of chocolate with a vegetable peeler. These can be left loose or wound into cigar shapes to make a receptacle for the Caramel Springs.

ice creams, sorbets, and sweet sauces

Everyone I know — from children to grandparents — loves ice cream. There is something very sensual about the smoothest, creamiest ice cream that makes it a perfect medium for experimenting with intense flavors. And it can be what you want it to be: a scoop in a cone on a hot day or one element in a dramatic dessert.

Vanilla Ice Cream

serves 4

3 egg yolks
⅛ cup sugar
1¼ cups milk
⅔ cup heavy cream
3 tablespoons light corn syrup
1 vanilla bean, split lengthwise

1 In a bowl, whisk the egg yolks and sugar until thick and pale.
2 Put the milk, cream, corn syrup, and vanilla bean in a pan and bring to a boil.
3 Pour slowly over the egg-and-sugar mixture, whisking all the time, until smooth.
4 Return the mixture to a clean pan and heat gently, stirring constantly, until the mixture thickens to a custard. Be careful not to let the mixture boil.
5 Remove from the heat and leave to cool, covered with punctured plastic wrap to prevent a skin from forming. When cold, remove the vanilla bean and freeze in an ice cream machine according to manufacturer's instructions.

White Chocolate Ice Cream

Make as Vanilla Ice Cream, but omitting the vanilla bean and stirring 4 ounces chopped white chocolate into the warm mixture until melted.

Rum and Raisin Ice Cream

Put ½ cup raisins in a small bowl and pour 3 tablespoons rum over. Leave to soak for 2 hours. Proceed as for Vanilla Ice Cream, omitting the vanilla bean, and adding the rum and raisins to the warm mixture.

Coconut Ice Cream

Proceed as for Vanilla Ice Cream, omitting the vanilla bean and using coconut milk instead of ordinary milk. Pour 3 tablespoons Malibu (rum and coconut liqueur) into a pan, heat gently, and then carefully set it alight. When the flames have died down, add to the warm mixture.

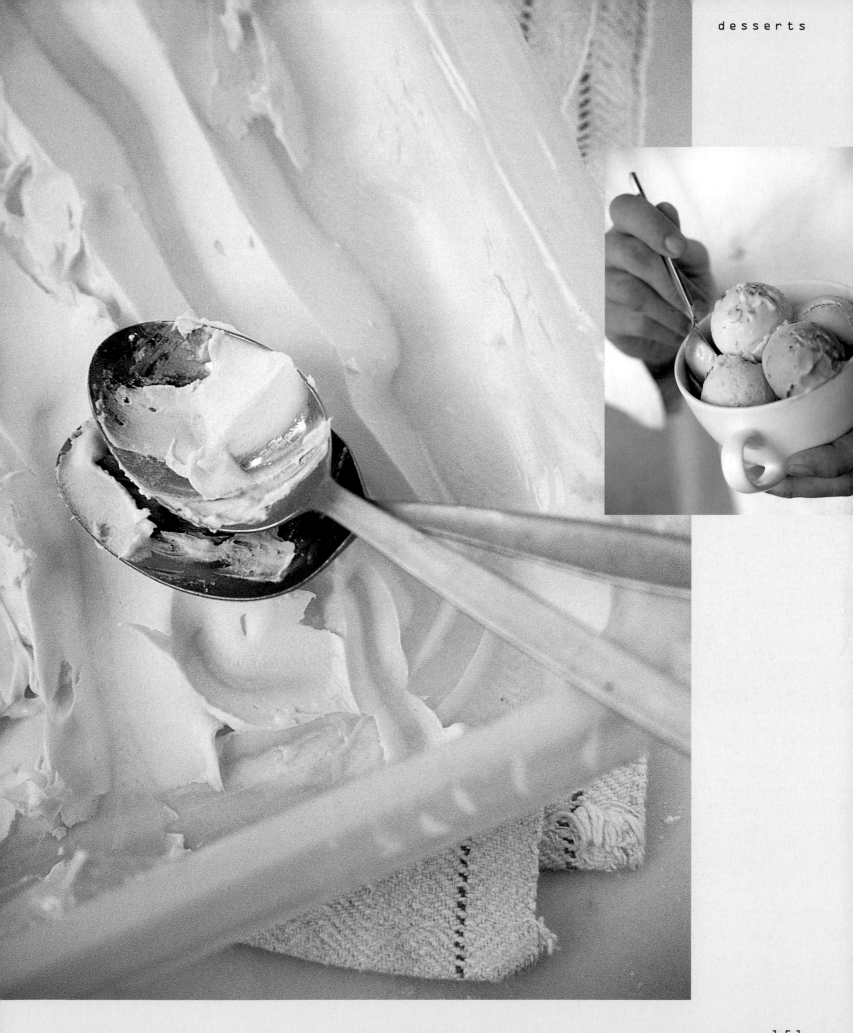

Strawberry Ice Cream

Purée enough strawberries to make ½ cup. Proceed as for Vanilla Ice Cream, omitting the vanilla bean and using only ⅓ cup sugar. Stir the strawberry purée into the warm mixture.

Orange Sorbet

2 cups fresh orange juice
heaping ½ cup sugar
½ cup light corn syrup

1 Put all the ingredients in a pan with ½ cup water. Bring to a boil (the sugar will dissolve).
2 Remove from the heat and leave to cool. Freeze in an ice cream machine according to manufacturer's instructions.

Caramel Ice Cream

Make a caramel sauce by putting ½ cup sugar in a pan with 5 teaspoons water and heating gently until the sugar has dissolved and you have a golden caramel. Add 5 teaspoons boiling water (take care as there may be lots of steam and splashing) and stir in well. Proceed as for Vanilla Ice Cream, omitting the vanilla bean and stirring the caramel into the cooled mixture.

Calvados Pomme Verte Sorbet

2 cups apple cider
½ cup confectioners' sugar
5 tablespoons corn syrup
juice ½ lemon
drop of apple-green food coloring (optional)
2 tablespoons Calvados

1 Put the apple cider, confectioners' sugar, corn syrup, and lemon juice in a pan and bring to a boil (the sugar will dissolve). Remove from the heat and stir in the food coloring, if you are using it.
2 Heat the Calvados in a pan and then carefully set it alight, to flambé. When the flames have died down, add the Calvados to the pan containing the apple cider.
3 Leave to cool and then freeze in an ice cream machine.

White Chocolate Sauce

serves 6

4 egg yolks
¼ cup sugar
1¾ cups milk
1½ ounces white chocolate, thinly sliced

1 In a bowl, beat together the egg yolks and sugar until pale and thick.
2 Bring the milk to a boil in a pan, then pour it over the egg-and-sugar mixture, stirring.
3 Place the bowl over a pan of simmering water and stir until the mixture reaches a saucelike consistency. Remove from the heat.
4 Add the white chocolate and stir until melted and well mixed in. Pass through a fine sieve.
5 Allow to cool, covered with punctured plastic wrap to prevent a skin from forming, then chill.

Dark Chocolate Sauce

serves 6

heaping ½ cup sugar
scant ½ cup unsweetened cocoa powder
½ cup heavy cream

1 Put all the ingredients in a pan with 1¼ cups water, bring to a boil, and cook gently over a low heat until the mixture thickens to a consistency like light cream. Pass through a fine sieve.
2 Allow to cool and then chill as above.

Crème Anglaise

serves 4-6

3 egg yolks
2 tablespoons sugar
1 cup milk
½ vanilla bean

1 In a bowl, beat together the egg yolks and sugar.

2 Put the milk and vanilla bean in a pan and bring to a boil. Pour onto the egg-and-sugar mixture, stirring well.

3 Pour the mixture into a clean pan, return to the heat, and cook gently, stirring, until the mixture thickens to a pouring consistency. Strain through a fine sieve.

4 Allow to cool as for the chocolate sauces opposite.

Coffee Sauce

serves 4-6

Make in the same way as Crème Anglaise, but add 1 teaspoon of ground coffee beans dissolved in a little boiling water.

Caramel Sauce

serves 4-6

1 cup sugar
½ cup boiling water

1 Put the sugar in a pan with ½ cup water and heat gently until the sugar dissolves.

2 Continue cooking gently until you have a thick, golden caramel.

3 Remove from heat and pour in the boiling water, taking great care as there will be lots of steam and splashing. Allow to cool.

Brandy Snap Baskets

The brandy snap mixture, like *tuile,* is pliable when it is warm and can be fashioned into any shape you choose: the classic way is to roll it up like cigars and then fill each one with whipped cream. I like to mold the mixture into baskets in which we then serve desserts of fruit and ice cream or sorbet.

makes 4

1 cup (2 sticks) plus 2 tablespoons
   unsalted butter
1 cup superfine sugar
2 cups all-purpose flour
1 tablespoon ground ginger
¾ cup light corn syrup

1 Preheat the oven to 350°F.

2 Put the butter in a saucepan and melt gently. Reserve.

3 Put the sugar, flour, and ginger into a food processor and begin to mix at low speed. Gradually add the corn syrup, followed by the melted butter, and continue to process until all the butter is incorporated.

4 Divide the mixture into 4 rounds about 4 inches apart on a nonstick baking sheet. Flatten each round with the palm of your hand, to form four 5-inch circles.

5 Bake in the oven for 5–8 minutes, until golden.

6 Remove the sheet from the oven and leave to cool for a moment, until you can safely handle the brandy snaps. Press each one into a soup bowl or over-sized teacup and leave until cool and crisp. Unmold to use the "baskets" for holding fruit and/or ice cream.

bread
puddings

Most cultures have a tradition of cooking with bread, born out of poverty, but humble puddings like the French *pain perdu* (French toast), or bread pudding, can also be elevated into something richer and more special — particularly if you use brioche as your base.

Brioche

As a child I used to walk past the local bakery and *pâtisserie* in the early morning. The windows were all lit up, you could smell the yeast, and there was an ambience and a buzz about the place. When I was fourteen I worked there part-time and since then I have never failed to be seduced by the aromas of bread straight from the oven.

However, a chef and a baker have different temperaments. A baker needs to be calm, relaxed, and responsive to the dough; me, I am always impatient, I like a fast pace. When you try this recipe, do it when you have time and you are feeling relaxed. Once you have made it you can use it, as we do in the restaurants, to make a luxurious *pain perdu* or bread and butter pudding.

If you want to make a whole brioche, rather than small ones, use a large mold and bake the brioche for 20 to 25 minutes. You could also make the dough using a heavy-duty stand mixer with a dough hook.

makes about 16 small brioches

0.6-ounce package fresh compressed yeast, cut into small pieces, or **1 package dry yeast**

4–4½ cups all-purpose flour, plus more for dusting

1 tablespoon salt

¼ cup sugar

6 large eggs, beaten

¾ cup (1½ sticks) plus 2 tablespoons unsalted butter

for the glaze:

1 egg

pinch of salt

a little sugar

1 Cream the yeast with a little warm water and leave for 5 minutes.

2 Sift 4 cups flour and the salt into a mixing bowl and add the sugar. Make a well in the middle, add the yeast, and mix together well.

3 Beat in the eggs, a little at a time, until all the ingredients are completely incorporated. The dough should still be sticky, but not too soft.

4 Flour your hands, then knead the dough slowly and steadily for about 6 minutes, lifting it toward you with one hand (you can use a dough scraper to help), then flipping it back quite firmly onto the work surface. When you knead, put your whole body behind it, not just your hands. As you work, keep sprinkling flour on the surface, and continue kneading until you have a dough that feels elastic and no longer sticks to your fingers.

5 Soften the butter to the same consistency as the dough, then spread it over the dough with one hand and knead it in with the other in the same way as before.

dough in each. Cover with plastic wrap and leave in a warm, draft-free place until doubled in size again.

8 Make the glaze: Beat the egg with the salt and glaze the brioches carefully.

9 Using scissors, make small cuts in the top of the brioches and sprinkle over a little sugar.

10 Bake for 10–12 minutes until golden brown (do not open the oven door for the first 6 minutes, until the brioches have risen fully).

11 Remove from the oven and leave to cool on a rack.

Pain Perdu

At home, when I was growing up, my mother often made this dessert with leftover bread and, sometimes, a little caramelized apple to go with it. I loved it then and I love it now. This is a slightly smarter version, with brioche, nuts, and ice cream.

6 When all the butter has been worked in, dust a large bowl with flour and put in the dough. Cover with plastic wrap and secure with a rubber band. Leave in a warm, draft-free place, at 68–72°F, until doubled in size. Punch down.

7 Preheat the oven to 350°F. Oil 16 individual brioche molds well (you can bake the brioche in batches (if necessary) and put a ball of

serves 4

4 thick slices of Brioche (page 154)

4½ cups milk

¾ cup sugar

1 vanilla bean, cut lengthwise into 4 strips

1 cup walnut halves

⅔ cup pistachio nuts

⅔ cup skinned hazelnuts

½ cup golden raisins

Vanilla Ice Cream (page 150), to serve

1 Dip the brioche briefly in the milk to moisten both sides.

2 Put the sugar in a pan with 4 tablespoons water and cook gently until the sugar has dissolved and you have a golden caramel. Add the vanilla strips.

3 Heat a frying pan and add a little of the caramel. Add the brioche and cook lightly on each side. Add the nuts and golden raisins to the pan. Stir to coat.

4 To serve: Place a slice of brioche in each of 4 serving dishes, pour on the rest of the caramel sauce, and decorate with the nuts and raisins. Add a scoop of vanilla ice cream and garnish with a strip of vanilla.

Bread and Butter Pudding

To finish, a crazy Frenchman's version of a very Anglo-Saxon dessert. Of course, you do not need to spin globes of caramel for decoration or even add my trio of sauces... You can even use soft white bread rather than brioche (increasing the raw brown sugar to ²/₃ cup), although the brioche just makes it a little richer...but why not end as I hope you began this book, in a spirit of adventure?

serves 4

for the simple syrup:

scant 1 cup superfine sugar

½ cup chopped dried apricots

3 tablespoons kirsch

½ cup mixed dark raisins and golden raisins

3 tablespoons rum

about 3 tablespoons butter

1 apple, peeled, cored, and diced

3 tablespoons Calvados

8 slices of Brioche (pages 155–6)

1 teaspoon ground cinnamon

1 tablespoon raw brown sugar

1¼ cups milk

½ vanilla bean

2 eggs, plus 1 extra yolk

½ cup granulated sugar

for decoration (optional):

Crème Anglaise (page 153)

Dark Chocolate Sauce (page 152)

Caramel Sauce (page 153)

Caramel (page 17), spun free-hand into a globe
    shape rather than springs

the night before:

1 Make the simple syrup: Put the sugar in a
pan with 2¾ cups water, stir to dissolve, and
bring to a boil. Remove from the heat. Pour
half into a separate pan.

2 To one pan add the dried apricots and
kirsch. To the other, add both types of raisins
and the rum. Boil up each pan, then remove
from the heat, cover, and leave to stand
overnight. Strain before using.

next day:

3 Preheat the oven to 350°F.

4 Heat 1 tablespoon of the butter in a saucepan
and sweat the diced apple until just soft.

5 Add the Calvados and bubble up until the
contents of the pan are reduced to a purée.
Reserve.

6 Spread the brioche slices thinly on
both sides with butter and cut them into
cubes. Put into a bowl with the apricots,

raisins, apple, cinnamon, and brown sugar.

7 Put the milk and half vanilla bean into a
pan and bring to a boil.

8 In another bowl, mix together the eggs, egg
yolk, and granulated sugar until pale. Pour the
milk slowly over the egg-and-sugar mixture,
beating all the time, until smooth. Pass through
a fine sieve and add to the bowl containing the
brioche and fruit. Stir to combine well.

9 Butter four 5-ounce dariole or timbale molds,
or ovenproof ramekins and divide the mixture
among them.

10 Place the molds in a baking pan and half fill
with hot water. Bake for about 30 minutes, until
golden brown and well risen.

11 To serve: Turn the puddings out of their
molds and serve with the three sauces. Decorate
with spun caramel.

index

acknowledgments

To my spiritual brother Marco – thank you for your vision, support, and help over so many years – and to my family, who gave me a good start. A big thank-you to all who have contributed to the making of this book – in particular: everyone at Quadrille, especially Mary Evans for her art direction; editor Lewis Esson, and designer Paul Welti; Sheila Keating, a long-time friend who came up with the theme and helped turn my thoughts into words; and Jean Cazals, probably the only photographer who can make me laugh under pressure.

Special thanks to my PR, Maureen Mills of Network London, who helped bring me out of the shadows into the spotlight, with patience, humor, and belief; and, among all the journalists who have supported me, Jonathan Meades – the first critic to single me out.

This book is not just about me, it is about a team, especially my loyal band of chefs/directors in the picture above who joined me from The Four Seasons to take a gamble on launching Maison Novelli: (from left to right, back) Jean-Marie Lenfant (Le Moulin de Jean, Brecey, Normandy), Mike Bird (Head Chef, Novelli W8), Richard Guest (Group Executive Chef), Duncan Impey (Group Pastry Chef), (front left) Nick Wilson (Head Chef, Les Saveurs de Jean-Christophe Novelli).

Also thanks to George Jardine (Executive Chef, Novelli at The Cellars, Cape Town), Jason Ward (Sous-Chef, Maison Novelli) and Chris Wheeler, my assistant, who has been like a brother to me, Igor Timchishin (Head Chef, Novelli EC1), my brother Anthony, Vicky Guest (Head of Reservations), Andy Phillips (Financial Director) and his team; Pascal Risso (Group Front of House Manager and design guru), Howard Linskey (Marketing and Operations Director), Jeanne Monchovet (Internal Public Relations), Xavier Chapelou (Group Wine Purchaser), Nikki Curtis (Personnel Manager), Ian Finnan, Dave Roberts and his team, and every single member of staff.

In the restaurant business good buying is fifty percent of the success, and I am lucky to have great suppliers, especially my long-time friend Bobby Lee at Daily Fish.

Thanks, too, to Liz McGrath, Fredrik Aspegren, and all the team at The Cellars in Cape Town, my friends at SeaFrance, and all my previous employers (even those who gave me the sack!), as well as the following people I have worked with or for, over the years: the Elie de Rothschild family, the old Chewton Glen team, especially Pierre Chevillard, Dominic Prandi, Alain Rocher; Denis Sirries, Gerard Basset, Giuseppe Vurchio, Neil Saunders, Nick and Sally Trant, Keith Floyd, Bill Stone, Fabrice Guihery, Robert Cole, Françoise Peretti and her team, Chris Watson, Per Redhead, Filip Tibos, Mike Ouchbakou, Chris Thompson, Ramon Pajares, Robert Cima, Karen Earp, Vinicio Paolini and his team, Rory Purcell, Nigel Firth, Colin Short, Jimmy Lahoud, Michele Andjel, Jon Gall and Jo Langridge from NatWest, Perry Lewis, Simone Kilka, Sarah Webb, Catey Hillier, Susan Duncan, David Pritchard, Yves Sauboua, Nick Grimshaw, Sarah Lewis, Claude Douard, Andrew Nurnberg, Trevor Hughes, Marcus Steel, Jean Louis Farjot, Olivier Poivre d'Avor, David Boland, Joachim Schafheitle, and many more.

I have to thank God for giving me all my five senses, the people who helped me to understand how to use them, those who appreciate them, and those who join with me to try to use them to perfection – whether it is in the kitchen, in business, in love... on all parts of the planet. Success is based on where you stand today, not yesterday, not just where you came from, but where you are heading. I will always be proud to be French, but coming to Britain was my only chance to be myself, and I won't forget all the people whose company I have enjoyed and who have helped me on my way in this country – from the day I arrived with nothing but two suitcases and a packet of Gitanes. I believe success comes from a combination of elements: shared creativity, honesty, loyalty, respect, and passion, so thanks to everyone who has helped and supported me personally and whose energy and hard work have contributed to the success of the Novelli Group. Above all, thanks to those who, through the best and worst of times, will still be my friends tomorrow. You know who you are and how I feel about you.

Finally, a big thank-you to all my customers. I will always have time for you!

A percentage of proceeds from this book will go to SOS Children and the Red Cross Hospital, Cape Town, of which I am a patron – not because I have a huge heart, but because those kids need help and they are the future.   JCN